CARSTEN THIEDE

The Heritage of the First Christians

Translated by Knut Hein

A LION BOOK

Oxford · Batavia · Sydney

Title page photograph: Mosaic of Christ from
Hinton St Mary, Dorset

Copyright © 1992 R Brockhaus Verlag
Wuppertal und Zürich
Translation copyright © 1992 Knut Hein

Published by
Lion Publishing plc
Sandy Lane West, Oxford, England
ISBN 0 7459 2544 8
Albatross Books Pty Ltd
PO Box 320, Sutherland, NSW 2232, Australia
ISBN 0 7324 0629 3

First published in German as *Funde, Fakten,
Fährtensuche*
First UK edition 1992

Photographs by permission of:
Carsten Peter Thiede, Paderborn: V, 1, 2, 3, 4, 5, 9,
11, 13, 15, 16, 17, 18, 19, 20, 21, 22, 23, 24, 26, 28,
29, 30, 40, 41, 42, 43, 46, 47, 48, 49, 50, 51, 52, 53,
55, 57, 58, 60, 61, 62, 63, 64, 65, 66, 67, 68, 69, 72,
73, 75, 77, 83, 84, 89, 91, 92, 93, 97, 98, 99, 101, 102,
103, 104, 105, 106, 107, 108, 110, 111, 112, 113, 115,
116, 119, 120, 124, 131, 133, 134, 135, 136, 138, 140,
143, 146, 147, 148; Datafoto International,
Bunschoten: 31, 35, 37, 117; Pontifica Commis-
sione di Archeologia Sacra: 29, 46, 120, 121; Oliver
Kohler: 132, 136; Roland Sheridan: 81, 87; Birming-
ham University Field Archaeology Unit: 75; L & R
Adkins, Lonestone: 56, 89; Trustees of the British
Museum: 3, 90, 91, 93, 94; Corinium Museum,
Cirencester/Rex Knight: 85; Manchester Museum:
85; Dean & Chapter of York/Derek Phillips: 81;
Reading Museum, Silchester: 74, 76; L Stanley: 73;
Zefa, London: 59; Department of Greater London
(Archaeology): 59; Kent Archaeological Rescue
Unit: 57; Yorkshire Museum: 79; Museum of Lon-
don: 60; Erzabtei St Matthias, Trier: 39, 44, 45;
Reverenda Fabbrica di S Pietro: 118; Rheinisches
Landesmuseum, Bonn: 118; Benedettine de Priscil-
la, Rome: 119; Basilica S Croce in Gerusalemme:
128, 129; S Mitropoulos, Jerusalem: 131; John
Crook, England: 139; Bargil Pixner, Tabgha: 146; S
Couasnon: 137; J Wilkinson: 137; Dominicani di S
Sabina: 144, 145; Vatican Museum: 122

A catalogue record for this book is available
from the British Library

Printed and bound in Spain
D.L.B.: 33.673-92

Contents

1

Two Caesareas

At Caesarea Philippi, south of Mount Hermon, Jesus once asked his disciples, 'Who do you think I am?' And Peter answered, 'You are the Christ, the Son of the living God.'

This happened close to a place sacred to the god Pan. Here the message of Jesus came face to face for the first time with the ancient myths of Europe. Excavations have started quite recently at Caesarea Philippi, and in the coming years, as these are taken further, more clues will be uncovered about the significane of this cult at the time of Jesus.

There is another Caesarea in the Holy Land, Caesarea Maritima, or Caesarea 'by the sea'. This was the most important harbour on Palestine's Mediterranean coast. Here lived the first Romans ever to become Christians, here the apostle Paul spent his time of imprisonment before being shipped to Rome, and from here the first Christians journeyed to take the gospel to Europe.

The theatre at Caesarea Maritima, rediscovered in 1959. In the background can be seen what remains of the original harbour.

Beginnings and their backgrounds

The sanctuary of Pan in Caesarea Philippi, beside one of the sources of the River Jordan (*nahr banyas*). Nearby a temple of Augustus is being excavated. The cave-like opening in the centre below the stone block is clearly visible.

The Christian message probably reached Europe within weeks of Jesus' crucifixion and resurrection. Fifty days after Easter the apostle Peter spoke to a crowd of people who had come to Jerusalem in order to celebrate *Shavuot*, the Feast of Weeks. The Christian historian Luke reports that among them were pilgrims from Asia, Africa, Arabia, Syria, Crete and Rome. Apparently Greeks were not represented in this group, but it is important to note that Rome as the distant capital of the Empire is specifically mentioned. On that occasion thousands became Christians and were baptized. Certainly there were some Romans among them who returned home after the Feast. Therefore an early Christian community may already have existed in the heart of Europe at the beginning of the year AD30.

Why was it that the Christians in Jerusalem began to speak about their faith to Jews and Gentiles immediately? Why did not they first spend time evaluating this important matter? Obviously they took the Great Commission of the risen Christ seriously from the very start! They were to go to *all* nations and make *all* people his disciples and baptize them.

However, the Great Commission did not come entirely unannounced, since only a few years earlier an event had taken place in the north of Galilee which could now be seen as its basis. In Caesarea Philippi Jesus had asked his disciples who they thought he was and Simon Peter had called him the Messiah, the Christ. The consequences of this confession of the Christ are well known: Jesus gave Simon the name 'Peter', which means stone.

What he said next, though, is intelligible only against the background of the archaeological recovery of this location.

Christ versus Pan

The town known as Caesarea Philippi in Jesus' time was originally called Panion. This still survives in the modern name 'Banyas'. It referred to the town's main attraction: a famous sanctuary of the god Pan. In ancient mythology Pan was seen as the god of fertility and thus of sexuality. By the first century, that is at the time when Jesus and his disciples came here, Pan had

acquired the designation of the 'all-god'. He owed this all-encompassing significance partly to his name: *Pan* is Greek for *all*, as can still be seen in the modern term *panorama*, an all-embracing view. Another example of the influence of Pan is the word *panic*. Pan was thought to cause the apparently unwarranted flight of flocks or herds of animals, so the word *panic* has become a term for irrational flight in most western languages.

The sanctuary of Pan near Panion was a popular stop for travellers to and from Damascus long before Herod the Great built a temple for Emperor

The rock with the cave of the Pan sanctuary. Immediately above it is the big niche of Pan. To the right are several smaller niches. Although the inscriptions still exist the statues are lost.

Pan playing a 'Pan'-flute and dancing with a maenad (woman devoted to the Pan-cult); silver dish from the British Mildenhall treasure, about AD350.

11

The aqueduct near Caesarea Maritima built by Herod. The Roman emperor Hadrian added to it during the second century AD. Originally the length of the pipeline above floor level was ten kilometers. It ran a further ten kilometers in water channels and tunnels. The aqueduct was rediscovered in 1963.

Augustus nearby in AD20. Herod's son Philip renamed the town Caesarea Philippi, thus cleverly honouring the Emperor (*Caesar*) and himself at the same time.

Caesarea Philippi lies on one of the sources of the Jordan, the so-called *nahr banyas*. Jesus and his disciples knew this. He himself and some of the others had been baptized by John further south in this river. Therefore the location was ideal for Jesus' question, 'Who do you say I am?' for two reasons. On the one hand it brought to mind their baptism by John in the Jordan. On the other there was the overwhelming impression of the rock with the Pan sanctuary. This question and its answer had not

only a historic but also a symbolic significance for the further development of the Christian faith.

Hardly had Peter given his answer confessing Jesus as the Messiah when he received a far-ranging promise: 'I tell you that you are Peter, and on this rock I will build my church, and the gates of Hades will not overcome it.' Everybody who heard these words had the illustration right in front of their eyes: there was the huge rock monument with the sanctuary, the many small recesses containing the god-statues, and in its centre the big deep cave immediately below the main statue of Pan. Thus it should have been plain to everyone that Jesus was promising Peter that the time of the rock of Pan was finished and the age of the pagan deities was passing away. He promised that the gates of the old cults, actually visible in the statuettes in the niches, and the bigger cavity in the middle, would not be able to overcome the new faith.

A Jew like Peter may well have thought of *Sheol* in this context. Sheol recalls the concept of hell as presented, for example, by Isaiah, but Jesus connects the vision of the prophet with the mythology present in the pagan shrine of Pan. In every age there will be some kind of 'hell', but Jesus' followers will have the power to resist its threats. This new power found its first representative in Simon Peter, Simon the 'rock'.

Thus Jesus used this historical moment at an important and influential European cult sanctuary to announce his promise. Caesarea Philippi was chosen because it provided a unique opportunity to illustrate the challenge of the belief in Jesus as the Messiah to the pagan world of the Roman Empire.

Both Mark and Matthew are very careful to mention the name of the location. Many of their readers would have known about the famous shrine of Pan, and some might even have been there themselves. For such readers it was immediately evident that Jesus did not avoid paganism. Rather, he confronted it at one of its most popular locations. It was

not until later that it became clear that Jesus' challenge to the myths of Roman religion was of much greater strategic significance than his challenge to the religion of the Jews, because Christianity was to become the faith of the Roman Empire. It was certainly no accident that he did not leave his question until they reached the temple in Jerusalem. The preparation for the missionary commission to proclaim the Christian faith to *all* nations took place right in front of the sanctuary of the 'all-god' in Caesarea Philippi, thus indicating the coming decline of paganism.

The way to the West

When the gospel was brought to Europe during the years after AD30, Caesarea Maritima was the natural starting-point. The port city was strategically situated along the Via Maris, the main trade route between Damascus and Egypt. The Roman procurators had had their official residences here since 6BC. Herod the Great had rebuilt the town magnificently between 22 and 9BC. Today the aqueduct which is many miles long has been partly excavated. It is one of many signs of Herod's building activities. Recently, further remains of the temple built in honour of Augustus have been recovered. The theatre situated to the south is the most impressive legacy of Herod the builder to the modern visitor. After its discovery in 1959

*T*he temple which Herod the Great built at Caesarea for Emperor Augustus, his sponsor. Excavations have unearthed an altar for the Roman city-god. The upper podium was used by Christians for many centuries. Parts of the big library may have been located here. Later it was changed into a mosque, then, in the twelfth and thirteenth centuries, it became a cathedral for the crusaders. The picture shows two pillars with crosses.

it was entirely restored and today it is once again used for theatre performances, concerts and ballet. Historically it not only documents the splendour of Herod's building activities; it also illustrates the extent to which Graeco-Roman culture had penetrated these regions. No Aramaic or Hebrew theatre existed. Therefore the tragedies, comedies and other dramatic events that took place here were generally performed in Greek, and more rarely in Latin, though this did not keep the Jews away. It was normal to be bilingual or even trilingual. Jesus and his disciples as well as the non-Roman citizens of Caesarea would not have had any difficulty in understanding a theatre performance in Greek.

In the course of later additions a stone was built into the complex, which was discovered in 1961. The inscription on it shows that it originally belonged to another official structure, a 'Tiberieum' or building dedicated to Emperor Tiberius. It also shows that the man who made the dedication was none other than Pontius Pilate, the prefect who pronounced the death sentence on Jesus. Although Pilate is mentioned in several literary sources outside the New Testament—Philo of Alexandria and Flavius Josephus mention and describe him, and the Roman historian Tacitus mentions his name to date the crucifixion of Jesus—this stone remains the only archaeological evidence for

his existence and office. Whenever important events made it necessary, Pilate travelled from Caesarea to Jerusalem. For this reason he was in Jerusalem in AD30 when Jesus was brought before him.

The ancient harbour of Caesarea has been rediscovered by underwater archaeologists. The few ruins above sea-level allow only guesses about the building techniques of this harbour complex. However, it is already clear that this was one of the most efficient harbours of Roman antiquity. From here those Romans who had listened to Peter's sermon at Pentecost could travel home. Philip the Evangelist owned a house here and here Peter baptized the Roman centurion Cornelius, the first high-ranking Roman soldier to become a Christian with his whole household. The presence of Cornelius and his relatives may serve as another indicator of the spread of the Christian faith to Rome: individuals connected with one of the town's leading citizens may have taken the good news of Jesus Christ on one of the many ships travelling from here to Rome. Even normal citizens could afford such travel; the Roman Seneca, a contemporary writer, tells us that sea journeys were among the things which were 'sold cheaply'.

It was from Caesarea that Paul travelled to Tarsus. Later he came here again on returning from his second missionary journey. Here he was questioned by Felix and Festus and from here he left the Holy Land for the last time when he travelled to Rome after appealing to Caesar Nero as a Roman citizen.

What happened next

Not many traces of Christian activity in Caesarea have been recovered. Nevertheless we know that it became the residence of a bishop during the second century. In the third century the theologian Origen was active there and made a major contribution to the formation of the famous Christian library in Caesarea. In 313 Eusebius, who later was given the title 'of Caesarea', became the bishop. He was to become the most famous historian of early Christianity. At this time the library owned about 30,000 scrolls and codices which made it the largest Christian archive in the Roman Empire. Not far from its supposed original location the temple of Augustus was discovered. Among its remains are a few pillars with Christian crosses on them, which remain the last visible hints of the Christian past of Caesarea Maritima.

By the time Eusebius arrived here the Christian faith had spread throughout the empire. Both Caesareas had accomplished their strategic functions: one of them, located far in the north-east, represented the victory of the historical Jesus

*T*he theatre of Caesarea Maritima in its much restored present form. Here Herod Agrippa AD41—44), the king who executed James the son of Zebedee (Acts 12:2) suffered a fatal fit (Acts 12:19b—23). The picture above the theatre shows a marble relief with a tragic and a comic mask dating from the second century AD.

over the ancient mythologies. Eusebius, in the other Caesarea, turned again and again to this point in his writings. And that other Caesarea had more than once been the starting-point from which the gospel reached Europe. The majority of scholars today assume that the oldest Gospel, that of Mark, originated in Rome and reached the Holy Land from there. It would then have come via Caesarea. But if other scholars are correct in assuming that this Gospel originated in the fifties in

Caesarea, it would have reached the centre of the empire travelling in the opposite direction. Whoever is correct, Caesarea would certainly have played a key role in the distribution of Mark's Gospel.

This book also starts at Caesarea. The next seventeen chapters will use selected archaeological finds to follow the way in which the Christian faith moved northward via Rome until it reached Britain. There, in York, Constantine was proclaimed Emperor of the Western Empire in 306 after the death of his father Constantius. Following this event, the second part of the book returns to the Holy Land until it reaches Jerusalem in 326 when the church above the rock of Golgatha and the empty tomb was built. It was a changed Christendom that arrived there and encountered the traditions of those who had never left. It had gained forms and structures which enabled it to become the power which shaped the history of the West. However, it was still recognizable as the faith which had originated from Caesarea with the Great Commission of the crucified and risen Christ.

The harbour of Caesarea was explicitly praised by the contemporary Jewish historian, Flavius Josephus. Only a few ruins are visible above sea level. Remains of the crusaders' citadel and the parts of a pillar mark the area where underwater archaeologists have been active since 1960.

This limestone block discovered in 1961 contains the only inscription with the name and official title of Pilate. The text outside the brackets is still visible on the stone; inside them the complete restoration: [CAESARIENSIBUS] TIBERIEUM [PON]TIUSPILATUS [PRAE]FECTUSIUD[AE]AE [DEDIT] ('To the citizens of Caesarea this Tiberieum / Pontius Pilate /prefect of Judea / gave'). Pilate was prefect of Judea from AD26 to 36. His correct title would have been 'procurator' , which is what the historian Tacitus calls him; in the New Testament the Greek designation *hegemon* is used.

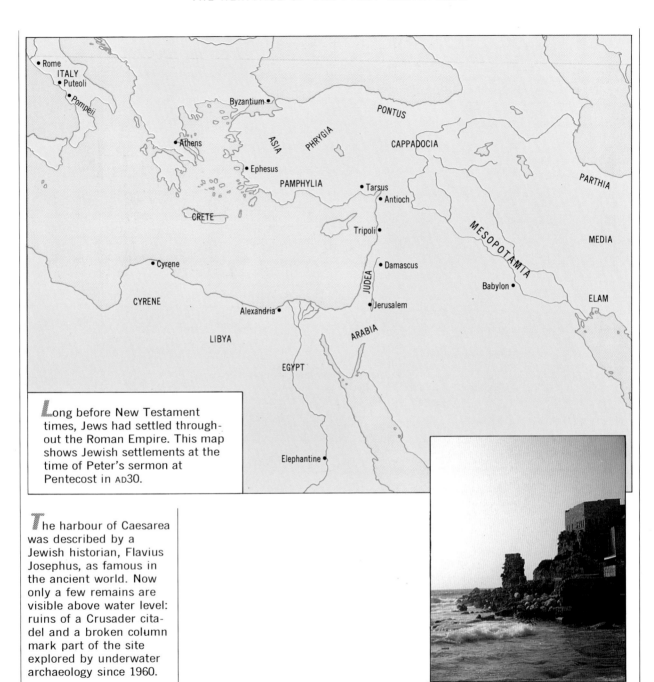

Rome
ITALY
Puteoli
Pompeii

Byzantium

PONTUS

ASIA
PHRYGIA
CAPPADOCIA

PARTHIA

Athens

Ephesus

PAMPHYLIA
Tarsus
Antioch

MESOPOTAMIA

MEDIA

CRETE

Tripoli

Cyrene

JUDEA
Damascus

Babylon

ELAM

CYRENE

Alexandria

Jerusalem

LIBYA

ARABIA

EGYPT

Elephantine

*L*ong before New Testament times, Jews had settled throughout the Roman Empire. This map shows Jewish settlements at the time of Peter's sermon at Pentecost in AD30.

*T*he harbour of Caesarea was described by a Jewish historian, Flavius Josephus, as famous in the ancient world. Now only a few remains are visible above water level: ruins of a Crusader citadel and a broken column mark part of the site explored by underwater archaeology since 1960.

2

Ostia Antica and the Roads to Rome

Many roads led to Rome. One of them came from Ostia on the River Tiber, the port for the capital. Excavations have uncovered an ancient synagogue here, the oldest so far found on European soil. The first Jewish Christians disembarked at Ostia, before completing their journey to the capital along the Roman road.

The architrave of the synagogue at Ostia Antica, with the 'menorah', the seven-branched candlestick. The support beams belong to the room where the holy ark of the covenant was kept, with the scrolls of the law. Although most of these remains date back to the fourth century AD, the architrave with the menorah must go back to an earlier building of the first century.

Travel routes

The Book of Acts explains how Paul came to Rome. He and his party travelled by ship via Rhegion Puteoli. Then they went through the swamps of Pomptinia on the Channel of Decemnovium to Forum Apii 37 miles outside Rome where a first delegation of Roman Christians expected them. Together they proceeded across country along the Via Appia to Tres Tabernae, about 48km south-east of Rome. There they met another group of Christians from Rome. The last part of the road led them on a straight line. Immediately before they entered Rome it was surrounded by magnificent cemetreies. The entire line of the Via Appia can be traced, but it is still difficult to follow Paul's journey in all its detail. Where, for example, was Tres Tabernae? Recent scholarship supports the assumption that it was near today's Casal Torre Ubalso. Unfortunately this compound is private property and no excavations have started there. This is all the more regrettable since the location is also mentioned in ancient literature outside the Bible and because it became a bishop's residence as early as AD313.

In comparison Ostia, the other main entry for people

The synagogue of Ostia Antica. A view across the different parts of the building dating from the first to fourth centuries. In the middle the central cult hall with the four Corinthian pillars; to the right the oldest part dating from the first century with the wall built in rhombic opus reticulatum style. Between there is the recess for the Ark, where the scrolls of the Law were stored.

travelling to Rome from the north-west and south-west, is much easier to survey and seems more promising as well. At the time of the first Christians this town was an important transfer point for all kinds of trade because it was only a few miles away from Rome and it was connected with it via a land route and the River Tiber as well. Here people met from all over the empire. In this context it is almost self-evident that just about every religious cult from anywhere in the known world was represented here. From a very early stage Jews settled here as well. They built their synagogues close to the ancient coastline outside the town wall, next to the city gate at the end of the north-south axis of each Roman town (the *Decumanus maximus*)—the 'Porta Marina' or Sea Gate. Between then and today alluvial deposits have pushed the coastline to the north-east.

The oldest synagogue

During excavations in 1961 the remains of a large synagogue were found in Ostia. Its oldest parts date from the early part of the first century AD. Walking through the town on the

Close up: two pillars with Corinthian capitals in the entrance area of the prayer room.

*T*he foundation inscription of Mindis Faustus dating from the late first or early second century AD. The text begins with a salutation to the Emperor: PRO SALUTE AUG(USTI), 'for the welfare of the Emperor'. The following lines contain mistakes in the Greek; at the place where the name is inscribed an earlier text had been chiselled out. The new inscription is written in a slightly different style. Presumably an older foundation stone has been reused by Mindis Faustus or the stonemason. OIKO-DOMES ENKE AIPO SE ENEKTON AUTOU DO MATON KAI TEN KEI-BOTON ANETHEKEN NOMO AGIO MINDIS PHAUSTOS ME DI(.) 'In connection with his extensive building activity and by means of his gifts Mindis Faustus has also set up this chest [ark] for the Holy Law [the Torah scrolls].'

OPPOSITE: *S*tatue of Serapis, god of heaven and the underworld, as well as the fertility god.

A small basin above a cistern which supplied the purification baths.

Decumanus maximus and leaving it through the *Porta Marina* heading for the beach, one stands right in front of the synagogue's entry left of the Via Severiana. Alternatively, those visitors to the synagogue who did not want to go through the town could reach it on a direct route from the harbour. This location, situated in an easily accessible area but outside the town wall, typifies the role Jews played in society. On one hand they were considered outsiders, and because of their strict rituals in worshipping only one God without images they aroused suspicion and misunderstanding. On the other hand they were accepted as loyal, industrious citizens who often received official privileges. Expulsions and persecutions were rare exceptions, like the persecution under Claudius in AD49, when the confrontation with the Roman Christians caused such disorder that the Emperor evicted both

Jewish and Jewish-Christian community leaders. Nevertheless, when the Jews in Palestine rebelled against the Romans under Nero, and Jerusalem and the temple were destroyed by Titus in AD70, the Jews of Ostia and Rome were spared any punishment.

The synagogue at Ostia demonstrates growing wealth. The many additions and embellishments which continued into the fourth century reveal self-confidence and influence in the Jewish community. An impressive testimony to this confidence is the central cult chamber with its four tall grey pillars ending in Corinthian capitals of white marble (see page 21). This is all the more astonishing as even in its prime the Jewish community in Ostia would rarely have had more than 500 members, though the estimated number of Jewish people living in Rome in New Testament times is between 60,000 and 90,000.

Only a few parts of the synagogue dating from its foundation are still visible, such as the remains of the floor, stone benches and a wall built in rhombic *opus reticulatum* style. The far right of the picture on page 21 shows these oldest parts. The menorah, or seven-branched candlestick, on the architrave (see description of picture on page 19) may date from this time as well.

A small basin (page 22) may perhaps also be traced back to the first synagogue. It is situated to the left of the main entrance above a cistern which supplied water to the purification baths. Some traces of these *mikvaot* dating from the first to fourth centuries have also been found.

An inscription from the late first or early second century is especially revealing. It was built into the first synagogue and then reused as part of the floor of the fourth century synagogue (page 22). Mindis Faustus, the only member of the synagogue's community known to us by name so far, ensures his remembrance on it and prefaces his Greek text with a Latin salutation to the emperor: *Pro salute Aug[usti]*, to the welfare of the emperor. The fact that the inscription is bilingual testifies to the reality that Jews could easily live in the a multi-lingual environment. Latin was the actual language of Rome and its ruler, but Greek was the *lingua franca*, the language of trade throughout the world, and both Jews and Christians could express themselves in it with ease.

The first Christians in Ostia Antica

The New Testament makes it clear that Paul and the other Jewish apostles always visited the synagogues first on their travels. Jesus himself had used the synagogue as the arena for his proclamation. He 'taught with authority' in Nazareth and Capernaum, but he visited other synagogues regularly as well. Later the apostles followed his example when they preached in the synagogues at Damascus, Salamis, Antioch, Iconium, Thessalonica, Berea, Athens, Corinth and Ephesus, to name but a few places mentioned in the New Testament.

There is no explicit evidence

BELOW: View across part of the excavated Ostia Antica. In the centre the Capitol, or senate house, in the background the River Tiber.

*C*hristian basilica dating from the early fourth century.

*M*odel of a multi-storey dwelling in Ostia Antica. In the early period the Christians in Ostia mostly met in such buildings. Often they gathered in the upper storeys which were disliked by other citizens because they became very hot and were often a fire hazard. Acts 20:9 gives evidence of how dangerous such upper storeys could be: one of Paul's listeners who had fallen asleep fell out of the third floor window.

for Ostia, but those cases allow us to assume they did the same there. It is certainly self-evident that individual Christians came through Ostia on their travels from a very early stage.

Actual traces of Christian presence in Ostia can be demonstrated only from the time when Christians were allowed to show their faith publicly in building projects. Consequently the Christian basilica from the fourth century is relatively modest compared with the synagogue. The basilica was erected on the same *Decumanus maximus* which led through the *Porta Marina* to the synagogue which was only a few hundred metres away. This may be evidence that an indirect connection with its Jewish origin was still recognized.

In addition, Ostia is also the place where the first Christian literary work in Latin originated. It is the setting for the dialogue *Octavius* written by Minucius Felix, a lawyer from North Africa.

Three friends meet for a walk along the beach of Ostia. One of them suddenly bows to worship a statue of the god Serapis (see page 23). His two friends realize that he has not become a Christian and a debate follows which is quite gripping even today. In it an emotional anti-Christian speech is set against an objective and level-headed defence of Christianity. The dialogue ends with the non-Christian accepting that he has been defeated, but that he has won a victory at the same time, for he has overcome his own disbelief.

With this small literary masterpiece set in Ostia, Christian literature in Latin begins, and here archaeology over the last thirty years has contributed much to our understanding about the context of early Christian beginnings in Europe.

3

Rome

By the year AD30 the Christian faith may already have reached Rome. By that time visitors from Rome had heard Peter's sermon on the day of Pentecost. Just as in the whole Roman empire, so in the capital city, Christians were not permitted to worship in public until the fourth century, so they met together in private houses. Because these dwellings bore no special marks of their use, it is almost impossible for archaelogists to identify them with certainty. But one such may have been a newly excavated house under the church of San Lorenzo in Lucina.

Stone blocks from the wall of a dwelling house from the first century AD under the church of San Lorenzo in Lucina, Rome.

Excavations

First-century Rome was fashioned by the building activities of Emperor Gaius Iulius Caesar Octavianus, also called Augustus. When he died in AD14 the boundaries of the empire were safe as never before. It was the period of the Roman peace named after him, the *Pax Augusta*. His forum, the altar of peace (*Ara Pacis*) and his mausoleum, as well as the remains of his palace on the Palatine hill are mere traces of his bygone power and splendour. For Christians Augustus remains ever present, since he is mentioned every year in the Christmas story as the emperor under whom Christ was born. Tiberius, his successor, reigned until AD37, and during his reign Jesus was crucified. One of the objects of interest for sightseeing was the *horologium* or great sundial erected by Augustus on the Field of Mars.

In the winter of 1979 the archaeologist Edmund Buchner of the German Archaeological Institute found remains which can clearly be identified as the remnants of this sundial. After careful calculations and in spite of an unsuccessful excavation earlier on he found it under the house at 48 Via di Campo Marzo. Among the pieces of the sundial was a 'travertine' or calcium carbonate facing. The block had

Model of the Rome of Constantine. Bottom left the River Tiber; at the far left is part of the field of Mars with the *horologium* or great sundial of Augustus (the obelisk is clearly visible). Below the centre is the stadium of Domitian, today's Piazza Navona.

a line cut in it for the months. In 1980 and 1981 excavations continued and well preserved parts of the sundial of Domitian were found. This second sundial had been set above the first sundial of Augustus, whose sundial was slow for several decades because the obelisk which served as the 'hand' was tilted. Emperor Domitian reigned from AD81 to 96 and undertook many building activities around the Field of Mars during this time. Among these was the *Stadium Domitiani*, today's *Piazza Navona*; according to tradition it was the place where the martyr Agnes was executed. He corrected the tilted obelisk and made some additions about 1.60m above the original floor level.

One part which is now open to the public is especially impressive. There is a network of different lines and well preserved bronze letters which make up the names of the signs of the zodiac. In addition a calendar inscription was discovered: ETESIAI PAUONTAI: 'The Etesia [the summer winds of the Aegean] end' (see picture on right). This discovery also serves to underline the importance of Greek in first-century Rome by showing that the language provided geographical and meteorological terms. It was the language of the first Christians in which they could communicate everywhere in the empire even if they did not know Latin, the mother tongue of the Romans.

Part of the sundial found beneath the house at 48 Via di Campo Marzo: the calendar inscription ETESIAI PAUONTAI, 'the Etesia (Aegean Summer winds) end'.

The excavator of Augustus' sundial stated that it was probably the biggest clock ever built. The line network extended 160m from east to west and 75m from north to south. The obelisk—the first one ever brought from Egypt to Rome—is still preserved and can be seen on the Piazza Montecitorio. Its actual height was 21.79m; to this must be added the two steps of the base (1.8m), a centrepiece of 4.36m and the ball on top. In the shadow of this impressive clock hand was a house which may have been used by some of the first Roman Christians.

In Lucina's Home?

The missionary strategy of the first Christians was to go where the Jews lived, for they still made up the majority of Christians, but at the same time to be where the people met, on the streets and marketplaces. Travestere, situated on the left bank of the River Tiber, and the quarter of Regola on the opposite bank, performed this function in Rome, as did the *Campus Martius*, the

Field of Mars. Among magnificent buildings Augustus erected there, the 'Felicula', the biggest tenement building of antiquity, was constructed in the second century.

However, multi-storey buildings, so-called *insulae*, existed here already in the first century. Most of them were situated north and north-east of Augustus' sundial. During excavations in search of the sundial, the first traces were found around the church San Lorenzo in Lucina. In spite of interruptions these excavations still continue, and frescoes (see page 28), a mosaic floor (page 29) and a later wall complex built in *opus reticulatum mixtum* style have been uncovered. According to the evidence the site was occupied from the beginning of AD60. The evidence also points to the conclusion that it was not only the poor (if any)

The wall with first-century fresco paintings beneath the church of San Lorenzo in Lucina. The picture to the right gives a good impression of the different floor levels. The building with the frescoes lies about 8m below the present church floor.

Black and white mosaic floor of the insula under the church San Lorenzo in Lucina from the second part of the first century. To the left a roofed water channel roofed. Possibly it was installed under Trajan, when the first hall replaced several earlier apartments.

Sketch of the tenement compound (insula) in the area of the present church of San Lorenzo in Lucina. To the left the eastern part of the network of lines belonging to the sundial.

1 Piazza San Lorenzo in Lucina

2 Northern insula

3 Via Flaminia

4 Ara Pacis

5 Via in Lucina

6 Via del Giardino Theodoli

7 Northern/north-eastern part of line network belonging to sundial

8 Eastern insula

9 First-century house

10 First-century(?) house

11 Early Christian baptistry

12 Inner grey rectangle: hall from the late first or early second century.

13 Outer grey rectangle: additional building from the late second or early third century; forerunner of the Christian basilica.

who lived here. Roman archaeologist Maria Bertoldi has provided evidence in support of the thesis that the site was not only used as accommodation. She dates the traces of a hall in the area to the time immediately after AD98 (in the reign of the emperor Trajan).

Further evidence is a kind of container which so far has been interpreted in different ways (page 30). Is it a water pool which belonged to the cult of the goddess Juno? Under the name Lucina she also served as the goddess of birth, so that she may have given her name to the whole site, 'in Lucina'. Is it an early Christian baptisterium, a pool used for baptisms? According to Maria Bertoldi it may even date from the second century. It is similar to the baptisterium in which Ambrose baptized the great church father Augustine in Milan on 24 April 387 (page 30). Is it just a round well with an overflow pool, as Friedrich Rakob from the German

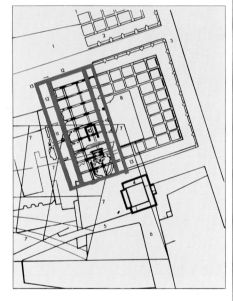

Archaeological Institute in Rome has suggested? If it did not serve any cultic purposes it would be more reasonable to suppose that it was a pool for distributing water, something which would have been very useful in an accommodation compound. The most likely alternative, however, is that it is a Christian baptisterium because it is covered with marble and belongs

Milan Baptisterium San Giovanni in Fonte from the fourth century (before 387). Clearly visible are the channels leading from the pool (middle) and into it (left).

San Lorenzo in Lucina. Segment of the partly excavated pool, probably for baptisms (baptisterium) dating from the fourth century, with a small channel for water supply.

to a floor level with additions made in the fourth century. Probably it belonged to the early Constantian period. Final confirmation may be provided once the excavations are complete.

The different opinions outlined above are characteristic of many archaeological discoveries. Many opinions must remain hypotheses. Thus there is still no consensus about whether the floor levels discovered under San Lorenzo in Lucina really go back to the middle of the first century. Archaeologist Maria Bertoldi's opinion is contested by archaeologist Friedrich Rakob who believes that they belong to the early or mid-second century, the time of Hadrian (from AD117). He holds that by then the *horologium* was no longer used and assumes that only then was it possible to build in this area. However, first of all it is not certain whether the sundial really did fall out of use before the time of Constantine. Secondly, it can

be demonstrated that building activities within the area were possible at an early stage, for even the *Ara Pacis* of Augustus was located within the complete network of its lines.

Did some of the first Christians in Rome live on the field of Mars as early as the time of Nero (AD54–68)? So far, this question cannot be settled beyond doubt. However, this location is one of the so-called *Tituli* (one of the earliest Christian meeting places named after individuals). Additionally, Roman Christianity claims that this site can be traced back to a lady named Lucina, that it was the home of the martyr Laurentius who was executed under Valerian (253–60) and that Pope Damascus was elected here, 'in Lucinis', in 366. The archaeological discoveries do not contradict these claims, and they may give some support. Whether, according to other traditions, Peter and Paul lived here as well is an entirely different question.

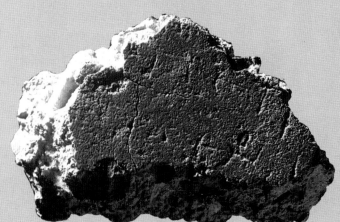

4

Peter and his Circle

'We know that Peter died in Rome under Nero—but was he ever there?' This jocular question betrays the controversial nature of many statements about early Christian history. One of the most controversial claims is that Peter's actual tomb, and even his bones, have been found on Vatican Hill.

Petros eni: 'Peter is in here'. Inscription on a stone found at the traditional site of Peter's tomb.

Santa Pudenziana; the south-eastern entrance along the Via Urbana. The low floor level, preserved in its original form from the fourth century, is particularly interesting.

Part of a house from the last century BC and first century AD with one of the arched openings leading to the housing space in the back. The streaks on the floor are traces of regular flooding through rising ground water. During the second century this was used for a bathing establishment, the Thermes of Novatus and Timothy who according to tradition are sons of Pudens.

Where did the apostle live?

No parts of Rome were closed to Christians. They could even live in the upper-class districts, since from a very early date high-ranking people throughout the empire became believers, like 'His Excellence' Theophilus to whom the two books of Luke, his Gospel and the book of Acts, were dedicated, or a certain Erastus, who was city treasurer in Corinth. We may assume a similar situation for Rome, although in this case we are lacking any precise comparable evidence for the first century.

Prisca, Aquila's wife, who was so highly esteemed by Paul (Luke uses the diminutive Priscilla), may have belonged to the old Roman nobility of the *gens Prisca*. But it is also possible that she had been released from slavery and, according to the custom, was allowed to use the name of her former owners.

According to tradition the present Roman church Santa Prisca is situated above the couple's home. In fact, excavations in the Aventine district, which was reserved for the Roman aristocracy, provided evidence of a dwelling house dating from the first century. This seems to support a well-born origin for Prisca, who then may have married a Jewish tent-maker from Pontus in Asia Minor and converted with him to Christianity. This, however, cannot be proved by archae-ology. Even further excavations would hardly be able to provide more certainty—door signs, entries in ground registers or a visitors' book cannot be expected. A similar situation concerns two dwelling houses which have been excellently excavated and which are also being associated with the whereabouts of Peter in Rome. They are the houses under the present churches Santa Pudenziana (page 32) and San Clemente (page 33).

In the first letter to Timothy a Roman named Pudens is mentioned, and later Roman tradition identified him with a senator who owned a house along the elegant Vicus Patricius (today's Via Urbana), where he offered hospitality to Peter. The latter is said to have baptized the senator's daughters, Praxedis and Potentiana. The large private house, built in the first century BC and expanded to two storeys at the beginning of the second century AD, is situated nine metres deep. The discovery of this dwelling house with four galleries in brick work and arched openings (see page 32) leading to several rooms dates back to excavations in 1894.

It is beyond question that this house was occupied in New Testament times. It is also evident that Roman Christians built along the Via Urbana in grand style soon after Christianity was made legitimate under Constantine, and amongst other things they gave it what is even now the most impressive apse mosaic in Rome (page 33). This all demonstrates the significance of the place in the chain of tradition. Is it conceivable that the relatively unknown Pudens, otherwise only known from among other names mentioned in a short greeting in Paul's writing, would have been chosen for a purely fictional legend? It is impossible,

however, to prove definitely that the senator Pudens accommodated the apostle Paul.

This difficulty of certain proof also affects our understanding of the origins of the church of San Clemente, in the valley between the hills Oppius and Caeliolus. Some people assume that the house of Clement was situated here, presumably when he was

San Clemente. A room of the palatial private house dating from the first century AD. The herring-bone pattern on the floor is clearly visible.

Presumed meeting place in a Christian house of the first and second centuries. In the background is a water-channel under a sloping cover. It is a branch of the ancient channel known as Fossa Labicana.

THE HERITAGE OF THE FIRST CHRISTIANS

On the occasion of the consecration of the church of San Pietro in Vincoli (St Peter in chains) in AD439, the empress Eudoxia presented to Pope Sixtus III the chains which are said to have kept Peter in the prison of Herod Aprippa I. The authenticity of this 'archaeological discovery' could not be proved. The inscription gives the Latin text of Acts 12:11: *Misit Dominum angelum suum et eripuit me de manu Herodis* ('The Lord sent his angel and rescued me from the hand of Herod.')

installed as Bishop of Rome by Peter himself. He is mentioned in Philippians 4:3 and copied one, perhaps even two, of the letters to the Corinthians. Excavations started here in 1858, and have still not been completed. The investigation by Louis Nolan (1912–14) was particularly important. He proved that a private house stood here even before the great fire of Rome in AD64, and that it was restored and enlarged afterwards. The building was a private house resembling a palace, as can be seen from two impressive rooms (see page 33) uncovered during the excavations of O'Daly (1936–37). Therefore it is questionable whether an unknown Christian could have been the owner.

Who was this Clement, then? Some historians have identified him as a relative of the consul Titus Flavius Clemens who was executed by the emperor Domitian (whose cousin he was!) because of subversive (that is, Christian) activities. Consequently it is conceivable that the Clement of the New Testament may have lived in the house of his well-off relative, and earliest church tradition seems to have known of these circumstances. The church which was built right above these rooms during the fourth century was not named 'Sancti Clementi', referring to a saint called Clement. Rather, it was simply called 'Clementi', without an attribute. During the second

*D*etail of the cover of a Roman sarcophagus, or stone coffin, from the third century. To the left Jesus and Peter when he denied Jesus, with the cock at their feet. To the right Peter is led away to be executed. This latter incident is not reported in Acts, but the scene carved here reflects Jesus' prophecy in John 21:18–19.

century some of the rooms below had been changed into a *mithraeum* devoted to the god Mithraeus (see page 33). But during the reign of Constantine they were returned to the Christians, and the church was subsequently erected.

When we stand below San Clemente we are certainly standing among remains of the first century of Christianity. Peter may have been here more than once. But again, it cannot be proved with absolute certainty, because the places where the Christians of the first century met did not have any characteristic features identifying them as explicitly Christian.

The 'Cross of Herculaneum' highlights this problem. It is a cross-shaped notch in the upper storey of a house in a town which was destroyed by the eruption of Vesuvius in AD79, just like neighbouring Pompeii. Although recent scholarship supports a Christian interpretation there are still sceptics who understand it as traces of a decoration attached to the wall, a wall chest for example. It is presumed that crosses had not been used by first-century Christians because the horror and shame of crucifixion was still fresh in their minds, although it may simply be that no first-century crosses have yet been found.

Chains, bones and graffiti

In AD149 the church San Pietro in Vincoli, 'St Peter in Chains', was consecrated. On this occasion the empress Licinia Eudoxia, the wife of emperor Valentinian III, dedicated the 'chains of Peter' which had been brought from Jerusalem. They are still

View of the left (southern) pillar of the trophy (grave memorial) of Peter. Bottom left is the wall which was built at a right angle to the so-called Red Wall.

Model of the trophy as it may have looked when it was built between 146 and 161. The asymmetrically arranged panel on the floor is of particular interest. Although the trophy is arranged parallel to the Red Wall its builders showed their respect for the actual tomb by this peculiar arrangement of a removable panel.

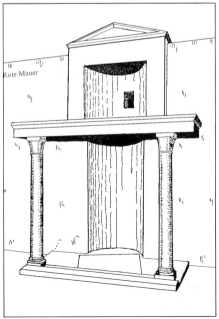

Rote Mauer

displayed there in a Renaissance reliquary (picture page 34). The inscription points to the original background: *Misit Dominus angelus suum et eripuit me de manu Herodis*: 'The Lord sent his angel and rescued me from the hand of Herod'—the words of Peter recorded in Acts 12:11 after his liberation from the prison of Herod Agrippa I.

This incident can be dated to the beginning of Agrippa's reign at the end of AD41 or the beginning of AD42. According to early church history and some recent scholarship Peter travelled towards Rome (which accordingly is the 'other place' of Acts 12:17) immediately after his escape from prison and arrived there in AD42 as the first Christian and apostle known to us by name. Consequently it is assumed that he returned to Jerusalem after the death of Agrippa, making some stops during the journey. He arrived there in AD48 and with his great speech led the council of the apostles to a compromise on the question of the Gentiles. He is said to have travelled to Rome for a second time in AD59. This must have been after Paul's letter to the Romans had been written, because he is not mentioned in the list of greetings there. He then stayed there until his death as a martyr.

Today nobody seriously believes in the authenticity of Empress Eudoxia's chains. Nevertheless, they have at least a symbolic value to remind us of the incident which led to Peter's first arrival in Rome. Different sources dating from the second century onwards indicate that Peter was crucified under Nero—probably in the last year of his reign, between 13 October 67 and the emperor's suicide on 9 June 68. Peter was buried at the edge of a large graveyard close to Nero's gardens (presumably the place of the execution), probably in a simple, undecorated tomb in the ground. Unquestionably the Christians in Rome will have remembered its location carefully.

At about 200—long before the official acceptance of Christianity—the existence of a grave monument can be ascertained from literary sources. The monument itself, often named 'Trophy of Gaius' after the author who mentioned it, was

recovered during archaeological excavations between 1940 and 1949 (for the south part see page 36; the sketch below shows a reconstruction). With the help of stamps impressed on bricks the structure can be dated between AD146 and 161. At this stage Christians were far from being officially recognized, as they later were, and only later would an interest have existed in inventing a tomb monument just for the sake of 'proving' something. In this case the reliability of historical, literary and archaeological tradition is unquestionable. An inscription on a stone of the adjacent so-called 'Red Wall' provides independent confirmation. The Greek words *Petros eni* are inscribed on it: 'Peter is in here' (page 31).

It is revealing that the inscription was apparently added only later, for the two lines drop towards the end and there was not enough space to write the

A wall with graffiti in the Christian meeting place under today's church of San Sebastiano ad Catacumbas dated between about AD 257 and 259. The big inscription *Paule ed* (which should be *et*) *Petre petite pro Victore,* 'Peter and Paul pray for Victor' is striking. Elsewhere is the inscription *Petro et Paulo Tomius Coelius refrigerium feci,* 'I, Tomius Coelius, ate a memorial meal for Peter and Paul'.

The oldest representation to be clearly identified as a picture of Peter. It was found in the catacomb under the church of Sant Agnes fuori le Mura. The inscription to the right gives his name in Latin followed by a version with the wrong Greek spelling. This drawing with red colour does not yet show the characteristic uniformity of the later illustrations on the early sarcophagi. Therefore presumably it dates back to the late second century.

*H*ead of a statue of Claudius, first century, found near the River Alde, Rendham near Colchester, Suffolk. During his reign (14 January 41–13 October 54) Peter first entered Rome and the Jewish and Jewish-Christian leaders were banned from the city.

*S*tatue of Nero, late first century, found in Baylham Mill near Ipswich, Suffolk. During his reign Peter arrived in Rome for a second time. Paul also came to Rome. Rome was burnt, the first systematic persecution of Christians occurred, and Peter and Paul were executed.

longer *enesti* instead of the abbreviated *eni*. Whoever added the inscription had to reach the Red Wall from an awkward angle. Roman archaeologist and expert on inscriptions Margherita Guarducci offered a possible explanation. The bones of Peter were in a chest in a hollow space to the left of the wall. The inscription was added only when these bones were deposited in this cavity. Under mysterious circumstances in 1942 the chest itself was removed to a storage room where Mrs Guarducci recovered it in 1965. The bones in it were carefully investigated between 1965 and 1968. They belonged to a stockily built man in his late sixties dating from the time of the New Testament. Peter?

Peter and Paul

The church of San Sebastiano ad Catacumbas is situated on the Via Appia. Below it a Christian meeting place used during the first three centuries has been discovered. Numerous bits of graffiti were scratched on the walls. Among them is the phrase *Paule ed Petre petite pro Victore*, 'Paul and Peter, pray for Victor' (page 37). The inscription probably dates from between 257 and 259, when the Christians were persecuted under the emperor Valerian. In particular, Valerian closed down the Christian cemeteries. In order to preserve the most precious

remains, the skulls of Peter and Paul were temporarily transferred to the Via Appia, Paul's bones being removed from his original burial place at the Via Ostiense, under the present church of San Paolo fuori le Mura. In memory of this short stay, the emperor Constantine erected the building which preceded the present church of San Sebastiano above the Christian meeting place.

After the end of the persecution the skulls apparently did not return to their original locations. The reliquary containing these bones can still be seen above the altar of the church San Giovanni in Laterano, although the first evidence for it stems from the eleventh century. A medical and anthropological investigation in 1965 showed that none of the bones of 'Peter' from this reliquary belongs to the bones from the tomb of the Vatican. However this rather macabre handling of bones may be viewed, the scientific analyses support the validity of the original traditions. A graffito portrait of Peter dating from the late second century (page 37) was discovered in the catacombs of Sant'Agnese fuori le Mura. Whether Peter really looked like his oldest graffito portrait known to us will certainly remain a matter for speculation. The claim that Peter actually was in Rome and was crucified and buried here, though, is historically and archaeologically well attested.

5

Going North:
Lyons and its Martyrs

The history of early Christianity was shaped not least by its martyrs and their testimonies. North of the Alps, Lyons and neighbouring Vienne were early centres of Christianity. Excavations have revealed the spot where one of the great anti-Christian persecutions, that of AD177, was perpetrated: the amphitheatre des trois Gaules in Lyons.

Arena of the amphitheatre at Lyons, seen through one of the side entrances.

A strategically important centre

As far as we know none of the apostles ever journeyed north of the Alps on their missionary travels. Paul had decided to head west, and there are many reasons and various lines of evidence to assume that he actually arrived there after he left Rome. Spain was one of the most fertile regions of the Roman empire for

culture and science, and both emperors and philosophers, for example Seneca, came from there. By contrast, the north was long considered to be difficult wasteland. Nevertheless, it can be assumed that merchants and traders from Gaul and other northern provinces travelling to Rome came into contact with the Christian faith at a very early stage. Indeed, obeying the commission to 'make disciples of all nations', Christians may have actively sought such contacts.

Lyons was situated in a strategically important location along the crossroad of important merchant routes and at the point where the River Rhône and the River Saône meet. Christian influences encountered here easily spread to other regions. Therefore it may soon have become the focus for towns along the Mediterranean and the River Rhône in the south, like Marseilles (*Massalia*) and Arles (*Arelate*). These towns were closely related to Rome, and as many of the inhabitants spoke Greek as well as Latin, the way was open for the gospel to be proclaimed at an early stage.

Beside other orally transmitted legends about first-century Christians in South Gaul, one tradition is handed down to us even in writing. In 2 Timothy 4:10 modern Bible translations refer to Paul's student Crescens who went to Galatia. However, some ancient manuscripts, such as the great *Codex Sinaiticus* and the great *Codex Ephraemi*

Expansion of the Roman Empire between the third century BC and the middle of the second century AD.

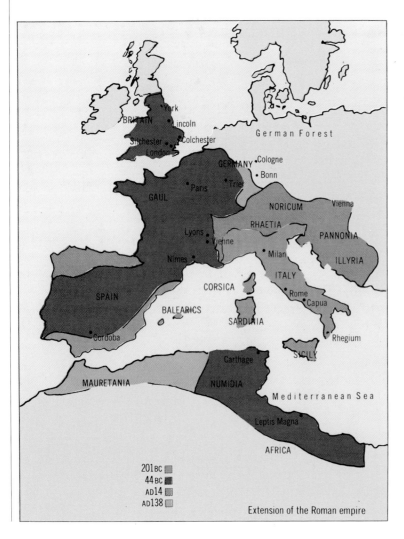

201 BC
44 BC
AD 14
AD 138

Extension of the Roman empire

Roman pavement in Lyons. One of the most important routes of the Roman Empire stretched from the eastern province of Asia with its big centres like Pergamon, Sardis, Smyrna, Ephesus, Miletus, Colossae and Hierapolis via Marseilles with its harbour along the Rhône valley up to Lyons and Vienne.

Rescriptus from the fourth and fifth centuries, as well as the church historian Eusebius (about 263–339) and such authors as Epiphanius of Salamis (about 315–403) and Theodoret of Cyrus (about 393–466) read 'Gaul' instead of 'Galatia'. This version was still followed by Constantine Tischendorf, who discovered the Codex Sinaiticus, in 1872, and the French *Traduction Oecumènique de la Bible' (TOB) of 1975 shows that it is not completely outdated; in a note on 2 Timothy 4:10 this very thorough translation supports the accuracy of the term 'Gaul'.*

It is impossible to confirm or contradict this verdict by archaeology or other sources. Nevertheless, there was certainly a big Christian community in Lyons, (*Lug[u]dunum*) in 177 for in that year a well organized and well documented persecution of Christians took place in Lyons and Vienne, including torture and murder.

An authentic site

At some sites where tradition claims Christian were murdered, the evidence is weak. At Lyons, however, there is no doubt the amphitheatre witnessed such cruelties. The eye-witness report written in order to be transmitted to the Christian communities of the provinces of Asia and Phrygia records the spot and the names of the victims: Maturus, Sanctus, Blandina, Biblis, Attalus, Alexander, Ponticus, Vettius Epagathus, Alcibiades and many others who remain unknown. Others had been killed in the *forum* or tortured in court and left to die in prison. Amongst them was Photinus, the Bishop

41

The amphitheatre in Lyons excavated between December 1956 and January 1958. The wooden post, front left, was erected in commemoration of the post at which, according to the church historian Eusebius, Blandina suffered part of her martyrdom.

of Lyons and Vienne. The names point to an international origin for some of the Christians in both towns who had Greek as their common spoken language rather than the local Celtic or the Roman Latin; the report of the martyrdom was written in Greek.

Irenaeus, Photinus' successor as bishop, who had escaped the persecution, wrote in Greek as well. Irenaeus was a 'foreigner' from Smyrna in Asia Minor, so the Christians appeared as an alien element not only because of their religion, but also because

some of their leaders were foreigners. Only one of the Christians is mentioned as being a Latin speaker: Sanctus. But apart from the confession 'Christianus sum' (I am a Christian) he said nothing and told his torturers neither his name nor where he came from. Even the name 'Sanctus' may not be his real name, but rather an honorary title ('the saint').

It is clear that the persecution did not start because of an official decree. It was begun by the mob and gained its own

*D*etail of the foundation inscription of the amphitheatre in Lyons discovered on 11 January 1958. In the first line the letters AMPHITHEATR are clearly visible. It was built in AD19 and dedicated to the emperor Tiberius.

momentum leading to the climax in the amphitheatre at the festival of the 'Three Gauls' (*Tres Galliae*) on 1 August. Although Christianity was considered illegal, Christians had not been persecuted officially since Trajan's directive to Pliny in 111. But in Lyons the directive was not followed. Firstly the Christians were hunted down systematically, then they were accused of infanticide, cannibalism and incest. The Roman legate, who had not been in Lyons when the persecution started, did not resist the demand of the mob, for once the Christians were in court their confession of faith and their refusal to deny it was reason enough to condemn them. In this he was supported by the emperor Marcus Aurelius whom he had asked for advice.

According to the law, Roman citizens were supposed to be executed with a sword while others were delivered to the wild animals (though the people of Lyons disregarded that, for they threw the Roman Attalus to the wild animals in the amphitheatre). This was convenient to the legate and the mob, for gladiatorial combats in the amphitheatre were an essential part of the big annual festival on 1 August, and in this way the Christians could take the place of the otherwise expensive gladiators in front of the animals. Eusebius who preserves the report mentioned above for us in his *Church History* mentions later that this persecution in Lyons and Vienne remained an exception. In the following year Irenaeus, who had carried the report, was able to succeed Photinus as bishop, to write his own main works and to send comments on ecclesiastical law to Rome.

The excavations

The amphitheatre in Lyons had been erected in AD19 and was dedicated to the emperor Tiberius. The hill *Condate*

*C*avity in the crypt of the *Hôpital de l'Antiquaille*. According to tradition it was the prison of the bishop and martyr Photinus.

The theatre in Lyons, discovered and excavated in 1933. Presumably it was here that the emperor Claudius (picture page 38), who was born in Lyons, made a speech in AD43. The speech is partly preserved on a heavily damaged bronze tablet found in Lyons-Fourvière.

(today's Croi–Rousse) had been chosen as its site. As excavations in 1974 showed, living quarters had existed there since the first century BC. In 1933 an extraordinarily magnificent theatre (page 44) and an odeon or concert hall had been recovered. On 13 December 1956 excavations started in the presumed location of the amphitheatre. On 18 December the first parts of the arena and the podium were discovered. In spite of repeated damage caused by damp excavations continued until on 11 January 1958 a labourer discovered a slightly damaged stone monument. The inscription on it is written in letters 25cm high and clearly identifies the structure as *Amphitheatrum*, thus providing the final confirmation of its identification (page 43).

Christians living in Lyons later selected sites for commemorating martyrs

Close-up of the theatre in Lyons with a view from the stage to the auditorium.

although often there was little reason for linking the sites to particular people. The crypt of the *Hôpital de l'Antiquaille* may serve as an example. It was erected on the remains of several Roman structures, and a narrow dark hollow can be seen which, according to the description in the report of the martyrs, was the prison in which Photinus died (page 43). Unlike the identification of the amphitheatre this is impossible to prove. What is important is the first evidence in Lyons of an extensive, hierarchically organized and extraordinarily courageous Christian community north of the Alps.

6

An Early Christian Centre of Administration:
Trier

Irenaeus, Bishop of Lyons immediately after the persecution, mentions Christians further to the east, in what is now Germany. Trier, privileged by its location on the River Mosel, was one of the earliest centres of Christianity. By the end of the third century, when Trier became capital of the Western Roman Empire, their traces were being visibly documented, as, for example, by the so-called Albana sarcophagus.

Sarcophagus of Albana, found in a crypt near the Abbey of St Matthias, Trier.

A fortified showpiece

Irenaeus mentions Christian communities in the Germanic provinces. In his book *Against the Heretics*, written about AD180, he does not note any place names but uses the expression *ekklesiai* (churches) which implies organized local communities, of which Trier is an obvious example. At the time Trier was the official residence of the Roman procurator 'of the Belgian and both Germanic provinces'. About a hundred years later, in 293, it became the residence of the Caesars of the Western Roman Empire. The so-called Albana sarcophagus, excavated in 1965, demonstrates the existence of Christians in Trier in the third century.

The *Porta nigra* originates from the time of the first Christians in Trier indicated by Irenaeus' comment mentioned above. It was the northern gate of the *Decumanus maximus*, the north-south axis of each Roman town (picture below). The inner side, towards the town, points the south, while the outside points north. With its original length of 36m, a height of 36m and a maximum width of 21.50m,

Southern side of the Porta Nigra. To the right the apse which was added about 1150.

it is both the biggest and the best preserved town fortification gate of antiquity. Semicircular arched windows and adjacent towers which bridged any blind spot made it a fortification complex without any weaknesses. At the same time the fortifications were furnished so ornately that this gate may also have served as a showpiece building to impress visitors from the north. The construction gained its name 'Black (*nigra*) Gate' only later, when the stones acquired a black colour through chimney soot and the influence of the weather. From the eighth century onwards many of the iron cramps, weighing more than 2kg, and individual stones, were removed in order to be reused for other purposes.

In the course of time the entire gate would have been dismantled and eroded, had it not been for Poppo, the Archbishop of Trier, letting the Greek hermit Simeon use the ground floor of the northern gate in 1028. Simeon died in 1035 and was pronounced a saint twelve years later. In his memory Poppo converted the Porta Nigra into a double church. When Trier came under Napoleon's rule in the

Northern side of the Porta Nigra.

The Roman villa von Wittlich, about 30km north-east of Trier. The central part with the arched entrance to one of the storerooms, which now has a modern roof, is clearly visible. At the bottom right is the River Lieser.

Close-up of the entrance to the storeroom.

nineteenth century, secularization did not spare the double church. The Church of Mary in the lower storey and the Chapter of Simeon in the upper storey were dissolved and Napoleon ordered all the post-Roman additions to the building to be demolished. When Trier came under Prussian administration, work continued until 1876 in the hope of recovering the antique original. The Roman *chorapsis* which had been added about 1150 was left intact as a significant testimony to the architecture of Lorraine in the twelfth century.

Important Romans, important Christians

The significance of Trier had already been recognized by the emperor Augustus. As early as

13BC he had ordered the systematic development of Trier. Its Roman name, *Augustana Treverorum*, goes back to this period. The road network provided ideal links in all directions: to and from Cologne, Mainz, Koblenz, Lyons, Vienne, Paris, Rheims and—of course—Rome. The emperor Claudius, who was born in Lyons, expanded the town in rectangular fashion and gave it the honorary title *Colonia*. Even in early times, at the beginning of Christianity, wealth and splendour had become a common feature of life here. Before his death in AD96 Domitian decided to make Trier the administrative centre and capital: *Provinciarum Belgicarum et duarum Germaniarum*, in other words the residence of the procurator of the Belgian and both

Germanic provinces.

There are impressive traces of both Christian and non-Christian life from Trier's first period of prosperity before the invasion of the Germanic tribe of Alemanni in 275. One of these is the villa von Wittlich which today is concealed by a motorway bridge. This example again shows the good location of Trier as a centre, but unfortunately it also means that further excavations cannot be expected. During excavations between 1939 and 1949 the remains of a farm complex with a length of 128m and a maximum width of 28m were recovered on the north east slope of the Lieser. The central tract, which today has a modern roof, is clearly visible (see picture above left). The entrance to a storeroom was also recovered (see page 42 bottom, left). The style of the masonry points to the early second century, but the huge, luxurious building was occupied until the fourth century. It is easy to envisage the scenery of the so-called 'pillar of the parents' in Trier in such an environment (picture right). The scene displayed reproduces the lifestyle of the political élite and the merchant classes. And it seems that Albana, the first Christian woman whose name we can identify with certainty, belonged to the élite of this period.

Outside the town wall along the road to Divodurum (today's Metz) is a large villa built in the

second century. Fine wall paintings and large rooms, one of which is a hall 17m long and 7.5m wide, reveal the owner's wealth. But the most spectacular discovery was made by archaeologist Kutzbach in 1923. After realizing that the hall mentioned above was an addition to the south-east corner of an earlier hall with a staircase leading downwards in the centre, he unearthed a crypt, 6.7m by 5.8 m. In the crypt, which was almost entirely filled up, Kutzbach recognized a sarcophagus (page 52) but it was not until 42 years later that it could be unearthed completely, in 1965/66. The

The so-called 'pillar of the parents' in Neumagen (Noviomagus) near Trier, third century AD. The picture shows a distinguished lady being made ready for the day. Sitting in the cane chair of a typical dining room she is served by four maid-servants. One plaits her hair, another holds the mirror and at the far right another is ready with a jar of oil.

West side of the Albana sarcophagus with rhombi and rosettes. Above, the dead couple are pictured at a meal served by two servants. They sit at a table and eat fish and bread; AD270.

peculiar style of the unit—the hall above with a single nave and its apse pointing to the north was reminiscent of a basilica, and the directly accessible crypt below pointed to a private tomb of a wealthy Christian family. The style of the crypt's building and the masonry both suggest that this tomb was built and in use before 270. This was 40 years before Christianity was officially sanctioned as a legitimate

religion in the Roman Empire. Only after the excavations had been completed in 1966 and archaeologist Heinz Cuppers from Trier had published his excavations did it become evident how extraordinary this find really is.

The sarcophagus of the *villa urbana* in Trier was almost completely intact and unopened. Inside bones were found which proved to belong to a man and a woman. The robust male body was buried first, and the strikingly delicate woman had survived him for several years.

The couple sit at a table with a red-rimmed plate with fish and bread. This is Christian symbolism, but also acceptable in a non-Christian setting. In this a careful balance was maintained, for apparently the husband had not been a Christian believer. Possibly his wife became a Christian only after his death. In any case the sarcophagus also displays pre-Christian symbolism. For example there are winged cherubs which are undoubtedly of Roman origin, for in Christian art angels with wings were only depicted from the eighth century onwards. On the south side dolphins are pictured. They can be found in Christian settings from the mid-third century in other contexts as well. Both cherubs and dolphins, however, belong to pagan culture. This cultural background of the husband may coincide with his professional status. On the gable side

opposite the death meal relief he is shown on horseback accompanied by two servants. The scenery and the white colouring of the horse point to him being a knight who may have held an official position in the empire.

On the basis of its style the sarcophagus could be identified as an artifact of sculptural arts in the region of the Mosel river from about AD270. This date is ten years after the persecution of Christians under Valerian and twenty years after the systematic attempt to wipe them out under Decius. It is hardly conceivable that somebody known to be a Christian could hold an important position in society or politics during this period. Only immediately after the husband's death did a time of relative peace begin when the emperor Aurelian came to power in 270. This interval lasted until the persecution under Diocletian (303–11). This coincides with church tradition concerning the woman whose sarcophagus presumably has been found. According to tradition her name was Albana. She housed the two missionary bishops Eucharius and Valerius and endowed the Christian community in Trier with property and, what is more important, land for a large cemetery. Above it still stands the Abbey of St Matthias. Five thousand sarcophagi were deposited here between then and the reign of Justinian I in the sixth century.

TOP: **N**orth side of the Albana sarcophagus. The couple on a rectangular background. In this picture the man is already dead.

BOTTOM: **S**outh side of the Albana sarcophagus. The couple on a circular background. In this picture they are both dead.

Christian Symbols

From earliest times Christians have used the

symbolism of bread and fish. A fresco from the catacomb of Calixtus (Rome) dating back to the second century confirms this. Bread and fish are reminiscent of the feeding of the five thousand and the four thousand. Likewise, these symbols recall the meal which the resurrected Christ prepared for his disciples at the Sea of Tiberias (John 21:13). Besides these there are other symbols which may have more than one possible interpretation.

In many Old Testament passages, such as Psalm 23, and many of the oldest Christian texts, the symbol of the good shepherd is often interpreted from a Christian perspective. However, is this always justified? Even before

Christianity, pictures of shepherds existed in Egypt, in Mesopotamia and in Greece. In Graeco-Roman culture even pictures of shepherds with a lamb or a calf on their shoulders existed, so it is exceedingly difficult to deduce whether such pictures dating after the New Testament period have a Christian origin. Are such pictures directly taken from John 10:11 'I am the good shepherd. The good shepherd lays down his life for the sheep.'?

This quandary is illustrated by the tombstone of the nurse Severina found near the church of St Severin in Cologne. It dates from the second

half of the third century, contemporary with the Albana sarcophagus. Its front shows the Good Shepherd and above it the neutral inscription *Memoriae* ('In memory of'). The two sides show Severina nursing and

putting a child to bed. Above both pictures is the text *Severina nutrix*, 'the nurse Severina'. However, apparently it was not the nurse but the child who died, although only her name is mentioned. The child probably died as a baby. It is pictured on the *clipeus*, the round shield which usually represents the dead. It is possible to interpret Severina's great love for the child as indication of her Christian faith. Such a memorial monument for a child is unique in the area along the River Rhine.

7

A 'Pious' Fleet:
Cologne and Bonn

The River Rhine was the most important north-south axis in Roman times. Along its banks, the colonists of the fleet and the legion built their settlements. At one stage, in AD89, the Roman fleet stationed at Bonn was styled 'the pious' by the emperor Domitian after it had helped him to suppress an uprising. Christians soon settled in this area, and among their earliest traces is the third-century memorial cell of Cassius and Florentinus found underneath Bonn cathedral.

Detail of the reconstruction of the *cella memoriae*, the memorial cell, dedicated to the martyrs Cassius and Florentinus, late third century.

An emperor as lord and god

The abbreviation CGPF means *Classis Germanica Pia Fidelis*, 'the Germanic fleet, the pious, the faithful'. These letters can be seen stamped on a building block of a building belonging to the Roman fleet on the River Rhine (picture below). The emperor gave honorary titles like this for special merit, and in this particular case we know the historical background. At the end of AD88 L. Antonius Saturninus, the governor of the Upper Germanic province, had conspired against the emperor Domitian. This conspiracy was crushed by the governor of the Lower Germanic province, A. Lappius Maximus Norbanus, at the beginning of AD89. The Rhine fleet stationed in Cologne distinguished itself in fighting alongside Norbanus, and thus alongside the emperor. Together with the other Lower Germanic troops the fleet was given the honorary title and used it triumphantly as part of its name.

Both under Domitian and afterwards this honorary name acquired a special meaning, as Domitian gave himself more exalted divine titles than any other emperor before him. He had himself called *Dominus et Deus*, which means 'Lord and God'. This designation must have sounded like a twofold blasphemy to Christians, for Dominus is the Latin for *Kyrios*, 'Lord', a title of Jesus Christ. Resistance to Domitian grew up in the senate and among the aristocracy, so hostile actions such as the conspiracy of Saturninus were supported by large parts of the population. It must have irked his opponents—and not only the Christians—that

Sewage channel north of Cologne from the second century. This part of the channel passes near the ancient praetorium beneath today's Budengasse, taking sewage into the River Rhine. It has a maximum depth of 2.5m and is 1.2m wide.

The abbreviated insignia of the Roman fleet on the River Rhine burnt into a building block. It dates from the late first century and was found in Cologne-Alteburg. CGPF means Classis Germanica Pia Fidelis—the Germanic fleet, the pious, the faithful.

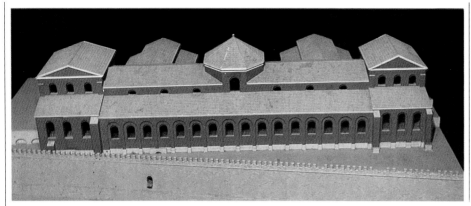

*M*odel of the praetorium, or magistrate's court, in Cologne, about AD180.

he gave the forces which defended him the qualities 'pious and faithful'. It was probably no accident that Domitian's assassination on 18 September 96 was arranged by a servant of his executed cousin Titus Flavius Clemens whose wife had been exiled. (Titus Flavius Clemens was a Christian.)

Cologne had become the residence of the Lower Germanic province (*legatus Augusti pro praetore provinciae Germaniae inferioris*) under Domitian. The oldest remains of the praetorium or magistrate's court (picture right) date from this time. Parts of the structure were found in 1953 when the town hall was rebuilt. Systematic excavations in the year 1967 and 1968 allowed the complete reconstruction of the building's history. It was not, however, always the case that a praetorium in the Roman empire was a building erected just for the governor. Frequently the official changed an already existing palace into his court-house and administration building. For this reason the

location of the real praetorium of Pilate in Jerusalem is still disputed. Was it the Fort Antonia? It looks as though this has now been disproved. Was it the palace of Herod? Or was it, as recent scholarship suggests, part of the palace of the Hasmonaean royal house of Israel, south-west of the Temple Mount? In Cologne the situation is obvious, for here a special building was constructed to serve the purpose. It was used as a royal residence and administrative centre until the Frankish period, under changing rulers and with constant changes to the building.

*T*he eastern wall of the praetorium in Cologne from the fourth century with a view of the remains of previous structures. In AD69 Vitellius was proclaimed emperor here. It was here that Trajan heard that he had been proclaimed emperor. In AD310 Constantine may have lodged here before marching to Rome. At the same time Deutz (Divita) was developed as a fort on the opposite side of the River Rhine. Only a few years later a Christian chapel was set up in the praetorium.

Current excavations in the quarter of St Alban in Cologne near the road Obermarspforten (see picture). View south towards the presumed location of the temple of Mars (before AD69).

Oil lamp with the head of Mars, second century AD.

Mars and Dionysos

Roman Cologne was called *Colonia Claudia Ara Agrippinensium* ('Claudia' after the emperor Claudius who raised it to the status of a colony, 'Ara' after the sanctuary of the local group of Ubian people, 'Agrippinensium' after Empress Agrippina because the foundation of the town is traced back to her initiative). It is typical of the atmosphere which confronted the first Christians in Roman Cologne that there are frequent traces of two seemingly contrasting deities. They were Mars, the god of warfare, and Dionysos, the wine god.

The significance of the Mars cult in Cologne is still to be seen in its townscape today. A road immediately south of the praetorium called Obermarspforten (picture above) points to the nearby temple of Mars. Excavations in the quarter of St Alban along this road are still in progress. They

have unearthed remains originating from Roman and medieval periods which also include part of a temple of Mars dating from before AD69. This could be the temple of Mars mentioned by Suetonius in his *Lives of the Emperors*, on the occasion when the Rhine armies

room of a house discovered during excavations near the south-west corner of Cologne Cathedral. It can be dated between AD60 and 80 (pictures below). The style of the pictures is comparable to fresco paintings in Pompeii, and they may have been done by Italian artists.

*W*all of the dining room in the Roman villa from before AD80. It was excavated in 1969 near Cologne Cathedral. To the left and right are two so-called shaded candelabra (after which such walls are occasionally named). In the middle above are the remains of a scene of dionysian or bacchic character

*C*lose up of the scene on the wall with the candelabra. A Dionysos/Satyr together with cherubs in a vineyard.

made Vitellius emperor in AD69. This temple also had a special status because the sword of Julius Caesar was kept here. The acceptance of a Roman deity in a Germanic setting is not surprising since the gods worshipped locally were similar. Even articles for daily use, such as oil lamps, had pictures of Mars on them.

Equally popular was the wine god Dionysos, more frequently called Bacchus by the Romans. Graffiti portraits depicting Bacchus were a frequent feature in distinguished Roman villas. In 1969 such a graffito was recovered in the fine dining

Cella Memoriae (memorial chapel) from the third century AD. Found beneath Bonn Cathedral in 1928. Today it has been partly reconstructed in the *Rheinisches Landesmuseum* (the official museum of the federal state) in Bonn. The benches for the memorial meal are arranged in a circle. In front is the partly preserved table block. At the back is the complete table block with the pottery bowl of terra sigillata (right) and the recess for the vessel (left).

Jesus said to them, 'I tell you the truth, unless you can eat the flesh of the Son of man and drink his blood, you have no life in you. Whoever eats my flesh and drinks my blood has eternal life, and I will raise him up at the last day.'

Rather than being expressions of worship of Dionysos or satyrs they served primarily as sensuous room decoration. The big Dionysos mosaic found nearby is similar. Nevertheless this deity was a particular challenge to Christians. The symbolism of the wine brought certain parallels to mind. While Christ called himself the 'true vine' and turned water into wine during the wedding at Cana, the followers of the Dionysic and Orphic mysteries could point towards the fact that their god created the wine and that he could make wine (and also milk and honey) come out of the ground.

How differently the apparently similar images were interpreted can be shown from another alleged parallel, which caused bigger problems to the Christians during times of

persecution. In its early form the cult of Dionysos had led to wild orgies (Bacchanalia) in which the raw meat of wild animals was devoured. The god 'appeared' as a he-goat or bull who was then consumed by his devotees. Already in the second century BC the orgies had been banned and it seems they were no longer practised in New Testament times. The problem was that the Lord's Supper could easily be misunderstood to be such an orgy and Christians were accused of 'cannibalism'. An opponent could easily misinterpret a passage like John 6:53–56 and imagine a cultic orgy in it, and a malevolent interpreter could distort such statements and use them to accuse Christians falsely.

The emperor is not Lord and God

As long as Christians did not get into open conflict with state authorities they were safe, even though they refused to worship different gods and believed in Jesus as God. Yet the emperor and officials constantly challenged Christians by demanding that they should offer sacrifices to Caesar. From such a situation arose the tradition underlying the oldest Christian discovery in the region of Cologne and Bonn. In 1928 a *cella memoriae* (memorial chapel) was found in a cemetrey dating from the first to the fourth centuries. It was situated below the cathedral of Bonn (the Roman legion camp Bonna). The style of the chapel (picture left) seems to stem from the third century, the time from which, for example, the Albana sarcophagus dates as well; current dating to the early fourth century is far too late.

A chamber of about 3.35m by 2.55m was found, and in it two table blocks, one of them only partially preserved. In the back two recesses can be seen. One of them still contains a clay bowl for offerings in an ancient death meal rite which was frequently adopted by Christians as well. Presumably another vessel with oil, water or wine was placed in the second recess. The bowl manufactured from *terra sigillata* (shiny red stamped clay) can be dated to the middle of the third century. Whether it was the original vessel or whether it replaced an earlier dish must remain a matter of speculation. Christians from Bonn seem to have gathered here, sitting on wooden benches which can also be found in the catacombs in Rome, in order to remember their dead in a memorial meal (*refrigerium*). Excavations confirm that burials still happened in the immediate vicinity for quite some time, despite the fact that the place was destroyed at about the turn of the

*C*ross 80cm long and 30cm wide in the floor of the hall above the *cella memoriae* (memorial chapel). It is made of grey-violet, white-red and white marble on the reddish colour of the hall. It dates from about AD378. It is directly above the cella and the workmanship is particularly fine. Its value and location clearly indicate the importance of this memorial site.

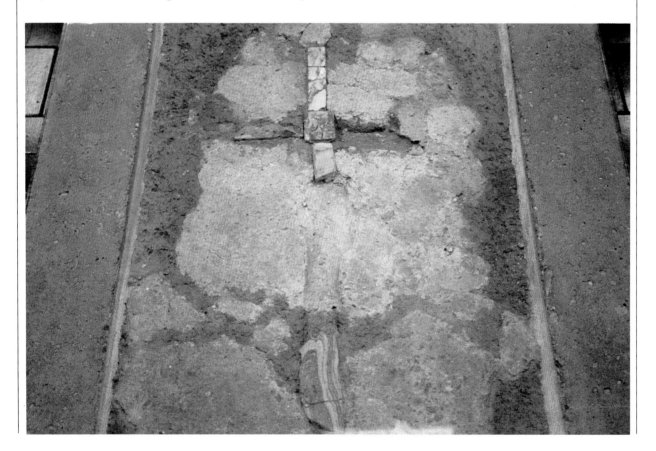

century. Interestingly, these burials were arranged as if it was desirable to be close to the *cella*. As early as the fourth century a hall was erected above the *cella* in which were more graves. It is characterized by a marble cross 80cm long and 30cm wide (picture left). There are three coins which give a reliable date for this section, since they were found in the mortar of the foundation. One of them was fresh from the mint and has the picture of the Roman emperor Valens (364–78) on it. As a result this unquestionably Christian hall reflects a direct continuity with the older structure beneath it. This local tradition was continued without a break until the Cathedral of Bonn was built in the eleventh century. But who was buried there?

The cathedral is dedicated to two martyrs, the soldiers Cassius and Florentinus. Thye are thought to have belonged to the Thebaite Legion in the military camp of Bonn (situated north of the cemetry). This legion, tradition says, refused to sacrifice to the emperor. Their martyrdom is best dated shortly before 269, the date when Gallienus, the son of Valerian, became ruler, since he was tolerant of Christians. Nevertheless, there are no literary documents which testify to the Thebaite Legion ever being in the region of Cologne and Bonn, although it certainly existed. The first report about the incident is ascribed to Bishop Eucherius of Lyons (before

AD450); a second report about the martyrdom of soldiers from this legion by Gregory of Tours dates from before 590. A soldier named Gereon was said to be one of the victims, and another church in Cologne is dedicated to his memory. Nevertheless, the two martyrs from Bonn, Cassius and Florentinus, are mentioned by name only in a deed of gift from the year 691/692. Therefore it cannot be proved by archaeology whether this local tradition is correct. What can be shown by archaeology, though, is the fact that a Christian burial-site in this place has been honoured continually since the third century. Along with the evidence from Trier this is a further indicator of the manner in which steadfast Christians acted in an exceedingly difficult time.

8

On British Soil:
Dover and the Roads to London

Even in Roman times, Dover was the main south-eastern harbour of Britain. Although definite archaeological indications of an early Christian presence are lacking, many Christians must have arrived here before continuing their journey north towards London, travelling along Watling Street, because Dover was the main port of the time. Extensive excavations are under way currently.

Parts of the Roman Watling Street still bear that name in the centre of today's City of London.

Names and legends

The Christianization of Gaul, at least under certain circumstances, can be linked to a historical disciple of Paul. In contrast, legends surround the traditions about the first century in Britain. One popular legend is associated with Glastonbury in Somerset. Joseph of Arimathea, the member of the council in Jerusalem who offered his grave for the burial of the crucified Jesus, is said to have come to Glastonbury. Apparently he plunged his staff into the soil and it changed into the 'Glastonbury Thorn' which can still be seen there today. Nonetheless, there are no historical and archaeological remains linked to Christianity before the sixth century. In AD43 the fort of the Roman fleet in Britain (the *Classis Britannica*) in Dover was extensively reinforced. One of the two lighthouses erected then is still visible today (picture below). This so-called *pharos* stands on the hill east of the harbour. Originally it reached a height of about 25m, and 13m of the original fabric still remains. It is the tallest structure of Roman origin still preserved in Britain and owes its preservation to the church of St Mary-in-Castra, which dates from Anglo-Saxon times, because it originally served as the church's tower.

Just as impressive are the

The Roman lighthouse of Dover (Dubris) with the church of St Mary-in-Castra.

rooms of a villa, the so-called *Painted House*, which was excavated in Dover between 1970 and 1977. The rooms are painted with frescoes (pictures right and below). It stood beside the road which led from the fleet's fort to London. Presumably it was constructed towards the end of the second century as a luxurious guest house for high-ranking visitors from continental Europe. Careful excavations recovered not only the artistic wall paintings, but also the typical Roman heating system which was unearthed almost intact. The heating system can be viewed here only through a hole in the floor. However, similar systems are more easily visible at other sites across the Roman Empire, for example in Rockbourne (Hampshire), Fishbourne (West Sussex) or St Albans (the Roman Verulamium, in Hertfordshire) in Britain.

In 1988/89, a similar installation was found near a Roman military camp in Bonn next to the River Rhine. Presumably it belonged to parts of the dwelling of the local commander, including a separate bath. Among other things some of the bricks on which the floor rested are still visible (page 66). Outside the rooms was a 'furnace' which supplied heated air. Coming through arched or rectangular openings, it could enter the empty space between the bricks under the floor. It served to warm the floor and could then rise through ducts to warm the walls and escape into the atmosphere. Especially in the cold climate of the North this so-called hypocaust system was widespread. The discoveries in Bonn show how this system also improved the luxury of Roman baths. Immediately next to the room which was heated by the hypocaust system was a bathroom (page 66) which was also heated by the hot air supply. Water at the correct temperature was carried by pipes.

The luxury and comfort of

View of room 2 in the Roman villa in Dover, about AD200. Through the hole in the floor in the centre parts of the heating system are visible. The main outlet in the front right also belongs to the unit.

Close up of the wall painting in room 2.

and Bithynia. There he was frequently involved in conflicts with Christians and in AD111 he wrote a report about them to emperor Trajan. In describing his country house near Rome he also sketched such a heated bathroom for us:

'Next come the oiling room, the furnace room (*hypocauston*), and the hot room for the bath, and then two rest rooms, beautifully decorated in a simple style, leading to a heated swimming bath which is much admired.'

Romans also wanted to be supplied with their traditional food. The typical kitchen was provided with all the utensils Romans were

accustomed to. Especially in the first two centuries many dishes and delicacies were imported from the south.

A picture (right) shows a typical kitchen in London during the first to third centuries. It was not until the late third or early fourth centuries that household articles were manufactured in Britain and no longer had to be imported. A dining room from the time of Constantius Chlorus (the father of Constantine the Great) was restored in the Museum of London as well (see picture). All dishes and utensils are originals manufactured in Britain.

Roman lifestyle in the cold north

Romans were not used to the cold temperatures and frequent rain in the northern provinces (Germania and Britannia), as written records clearly show, and the invention of a central heating system brought most welcome relief. A typical example of such a system is the hypocaust heating system excavated in Bonn between 1988 and 1989 (picture top left). (The expression 'hypocaust' is

derived from Greek *hypokaio* meaning 'to light something from beneath' or 'to heat something from below'.) It dates from the first century and belonged to the villa of the military commander in Bonna. Adjacent was the water pool of the bathroom belonging to the commander's house. The picture shows one of the pipes in the bathroom (centre left).

The Roman writer Pliny the Younger (AD61—113) was one of the leading officials in the provinces of Pontus

Roman housing in Britain can be seen in a kitchen and dining room from London reconstructed with its original furnishings (page 66). For Christians coming to Britain, the luxury enjoyed by the élite of the occupying power was not something unknown or foreign. Even amongst Christian merchants in New Testament times there were well-off men and women, for example Aquila and Prisca who owned houses in Rome and Corinth. There were also Gaius and Erastus in Corinth, one of them owner of a house big enough to accommodate the entire Christian church in Corinth, the other being the city treasurer. The house along the Vitus Patricius in Rome which may have belonged to the Pudens mentioned in 2 Timothy 4:21 has been dealt with in an earlier chapter.

On their way to London travellers also came through Canterbury (Durovernum Cantiacorum). Parts of the forum, the theatre, individual houses and the road system have been excavated and could be restored in part. Unfortunately the excavations around the cathedral (picture above), the seat of the head of the Church of England—the Archbishop of Canterbury—have not uncovered remains earlier than the fourth century, the time of the official Christianization under and after Constantine. At least there is some confirmation of the assumption that the missionary Augustine, who was sent to the

island by Pope Gregory in 597, prompted the enlargement and improvement of an older church at this site. It might have been possible to get more details, especially about the original building activities, by excavating beneath the present cathedral. Unfortunately this seems to be out of the question. The situation with two other churches in the town centre, St Martin and St Pancras, which date from the late Roman period, is similar.

Visible traces of the old Roman Watling Street are being unearthed through recent excavations in Southwark, a London district south of the Thames (picture right). At first remains of prehistoric settlements (about 6000BC and 3000BC) were discovered in the area of the Old Kent Road and Bowles Road between 28 March

Canterbury Cathedral with the remains of Augustine's building activities, about AD600.

Excavation works in 'trench C' of the Roman Watling Street (Old Kent Road/Bowles Road) in London, August 1990.

Partial reconstruction of the Mithraeum in London. In the background Queen Victoria Street.

The head of Mithras from the Mithraeum in London, about AD180; manufactured in Carrara marble, probably by an Italian workshop. Head and neck were found separately on 18 and 21 September 1954. Originally the whole face was as smooth as the neck and the right cheek.

and 24 August 1990. Subsequently Roman pottery, notably waterproof silicious potsherds, was uncovered in three trenches. Archaeologists believe that it belonged to the foundation level of the Roman road where potsherds were supposed to improve the road's stability and water drainage. Coins discovered here led to the conclusion that the road was constantly being repaired between the first and fourth centuries, until maintenance work stopped when the Romans withdrew from Britain at the beginning of the fifth century. Bricks used for building and a gem stone dated to the second century also suggest that there was a small Roman settlement nearby, possibly a small country house 3 miles outside the city gate. The course of the Roman road just outside London on which the first Christians travelled to the capital can now be traced with certainty.

An early competitor: Mithras

Wherever Roman soldiers lived, no matter whether it was in inland fortresses or along main routes or in the towns, one cult remained a major challenge to Christianity for a long time: the Mithras cult which originated in Persia. The remains found in London at Walbrook north of the River Thames near Watling Street in 1954 are noteworthy (pages 68 and 69). Although superficially the discoveries do not give many clues to the fact that this cult was a competitor for Christianity, a hint of it can be found in the architecture: the shrines ended in an apse just like Christian churches. The Mithraeum—the temple for wor-shipping

Mithras—in London, with its apse facing west, is an example of this. However, the real similarity lay in the promises of both religions. The Mithras cult promised personal salvation and life after death. It also included a 'farewell meal' and an 'ascension to heaven' of its deity. It was a less demanding religion than Christianity in that it did not ask its followers to resist the emperor cult, which caused so many persecutions of the Christians.

choosing the same date Christians could claim to substitute the Jesus who was both a human being and God for the pagan myth.

Nonetheless, similarities were only superficial and closer investigation revealed that every detail of the two systems of belief was very different. The cult of Mithras only addressed men, whereas Christianity was clearly distinguished from its pagan surrounding in giving equal

Consequently, it was a big problem for Christian missionaries because it offered similar promises without any comparable risks. It is even possible to understand the decision to link the date of Christmas to 25 December as a reaction to this controversy. This day was supposed to be the anniversary of Mithras, and by

importance to women in its offer of salvation. The followers of Mithras were required to go through harsh initiation rites. There were seven stages of consecration which were called 'Raven', 'Bridegroom', 'Soldier', 'Lion', 'Persian', 'Messenger of the Sun' and 'Father'. During the actual rites worshippers would focus on the centre of the cult

*R*elief with Mithras killing the bull (Mithras Tauroctonos) from the Mithraeum in London. To the left stands Cautes symbolizing light with a raised torch and to the right Cautopates symbolizing darkness with a lowered torch. A dog and a snake (only its head and the end of its body are still visible) drink the blood. A scorpion attacks the bull's genitals. The signs of the zodiac are engraved in the circle; outside it and above is Sol, the sun god, with his four horses, opposite to the right is the moon goddess Luna who sends down two bulls. At the bottom two wind deities are visible: to the left presumably Boreas, to the right probably Zephyros. The broken text to the left and right of the relief names the dedicator Ulpius Silvanus. He had left the second legion of Augustus and was initiated into the cult of Mithras in Orange (the ancient Arausio in Gaul). Carrara marble, about AD150.

The dining room (*triclinium*) in the Mithraeum of San Clemente in Rome, dating from the third century. In the foreground stands a small altar carved with Mithras killing the bull. To the left and right are benches for the followers of Mithras. In the background Mithras is represented, being born from a rock. The altar itself may have stood in the room opposite. The *triclinium* was used for a meal commemorating the farewell meal of Mithras and Apollo after his victory over the bull and before Mithras' ascension to heaven in Apollo's fiery chariot.

chamber with the altar of Mithras. On it were reliefs depicting Mithras slaughtering a bull, with his knife in the bull's neck (pages 69 and 70). The bull's blood was supposed to cause the vines to grow, and corn was thought to come forth from its body.

Frequently Mithras is depicted with his two companions Cautes (the symbol of light, day and life) and Cautopates (the symbol of darkness, night and death). Soldiers in particular came to equate Mithras with *Sol invictus*, the invincible sun god, Sol. Constantine the Great was for a long time a worshipper of Sol.

The Mithras items in London

are well preserved because they were hidden beneath the floor of the cult chamber, probably from fear of an attack—possibly by Christians—during the fourth century. The comparison between Christians and the followers of Mithras is most clearly seen, however, beneath the church of San Clemente in Rome (picture above). Next to the first-century Christian building, possibly during the persecution of Christians under Valerian, Mithras worshippers had established a school, a cult chamber and a dining room which make it possible for us to understand the nature of this cult.

9

London

London's early Christian past is not yet as clear as we might hope; too many potential traces may be lost for ever, some may yet be dug up, others are obscured by thick layers of legend. But the elements common to early Christian communities all over the Empire will also have held true for London; and thus it is underneath some of the old churches there that remnants of Roman private houses may point to local church traditions. All Hallows by the Tower and St Bride's, Fleet Street, are two examples of this.

Floor of second-century Roman house beneath All Hallows by the Tower

At the fringes of Londinium

The major invasion of Britain under the emperor Claudius took place in AD43. Because of its strategic importance the area north of the River Thames and east of Walbrook was fortified immediately. However, only seventeen years later Londinium fell to the uprising of the Iceni tribe under Queen Boadicea (Boudicca).

The town was destroyed and burnt down to its foundations. Archaeologists still find heavily burnt layers which indicate a major fire. After being rebuilt, the significance of the town increased. First it became the residence of the procurator and from AD197 onwards it became capital of the newly established province *Britannia Superior*. The remains of the Roman city wall north of the Tower belong to this period (picture below).

A view west from inside the wall catches the church of St Mary by the Tower (picture below).

Here, in the south-east corner of the Roman Londinium between Great Tower Street and Byward Street, were the houses of well-to-do citizens. The floor of such a house, dating from the end of the second century (picture above), was found beneath the church. The mosaic on the floor, traces of red-coloured plastering and a partition wall are clearly visible. There are no written traditions concerning its owner. However, in about AD675 the Christian Anglo-Saxons built a church here despite its location in the outskirts of the city.

Today its size can still be deduced from the arched door built with Roman stones and tiles (page 73 far right).

It must remain an open question whether this house was destroyed by vandalizing Saxons and Franks crossing the Channel in 367 or whether it was left behind by the last Romans when they finally withdrew from Britain in 410. In any case a local Christian tradition may have existed here which was revived after 597.

A house outside the city gates

The church of St Bride's is behind Fleet Street, about 400m

View westwards from Wakefield Gardens (the site of the remains of the Roman wall) to the church of All Hallows by the Tower.

Remains of the Roman city wall, with a length of 15m and a maximum height of 6m north of the Tower which is visible in the background.

west of Ludgate, the southern of the two western gates of *Londinium* erected about AD200.

Tourists looking for the old splendour of London hardly ever enter this church. Beneath it can be seen the remains of another Roman house which may have a Christian background (page 75). Already in AD43 the Romans built a moat in the area near the church.

Later, however, the city wall was built further east. In the second century a house with a street entrance was built close to this ditch at about the same time as the house beneath All Hallows by the Tower. Traces of it were found during drainage works following the church's almost complete destruction in a German air-raid on 29 December 1940 (page 76 left).

Parts of the road, a floor mosaic and a wall, as well as numerous small objects (page 76 left) were unearthed. Regardless of its interpretation, it is the only building west of the ancient city

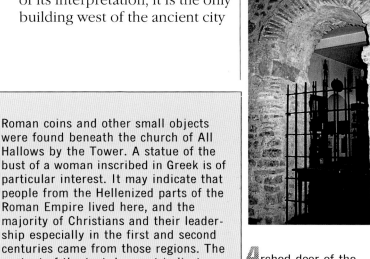

floor mosaic in a Roman house of the second century under the church of All Hallows by the Tower.

Arched door of the seventh-century church built on the site of a Roman private house. The Roman style of architecture and the use of Roman tiles are clearly visible.

Roman coins and other small objects were found beneath the church of All Hallows by the Tower. A statue of the bust of a woman inscribed in Greek is of particular interest. It may indicate that people from the Hellenized parts of the Roman Empire lived here, and the majority of Christians and their leadership especially in the first and second centuries came from those regions. The content of the text does not indicate whether it was written from a Christian or pagan point of view: 'from Demetri(o)s for Heraclia, his wife, to her memory, from her expenses'. Apparently she was a wealthy woman who had arranged for part of her assets to be used to pay for this memorial.

wall which can unquestionably be identified as Roman.

Here, in a fairly unfavourable position, a stone-built church was erected in the sixth century, linked to an earlier church structure built of wood.

Again, there is no written evidence that it belonged to the pre-Constantine period. Nevertheless it is possible to take the hypothesis that this was a Christian meeeting place in a

Entrance to the present church of St Bride's, Fleet Street

Roman private house a step further.

According to our oldest evidence the name of the church was St Bride's. St Bride, that is St Brigid of Kildare in Ireland, can be linked with Celtic Christianity. It can therefore be conjectured that a successful mission of Roman Christians amongst local Celts began here and that its consequences were still being felt in post-Roman times.

A copper nail and a green mosaic stone found here suggest a well-to-do owner, all the more so because this kind of mosaic material had to be imported from Italy.

From the possible to the unlikely

Old traditions connected with All Hallows and St Bride's may indicate that there were Christian private houses of the second century. In contrast to these another place is connected with a legend which arose from a misunderstanding.

The legend says that the church of St Peter's upon Cornhill (page 76) was founded by King Lucius in AD179. As a matter of fact the present church stands above the northern part of a public building of the first century, the so-called 'Basilica' which enclosed the forum and a temple. So the Romans did build here, but the fact that it was such a public building and situated in the town centre rules out the

Crypt of St Bride's with remnants of a wall from the Roman period.

possibility that it could have been a church.

Although Christianity was just tolerated at this period it is inconceivable that a church would have been allowed such a dominant position.

The error goes back to the Venerable Bede, the English church historian. In his church history completed in 731 he reports how the British King Lucius wrote to Pope Eleutherius and asked him to make him a Christian. Bede dated the incident to the reign of the emperors Marcus Antoninus Verus and Aurelius Commodus who reigned together from AD156. The two emperors and the Pope who was in office from AD174 to 189 did actually exist.

Bede did not invent this story himself, for as early as the sixth century the Roman *Liber Pontificalis* tells the story of Lucius and his letter.

However, the actual error can be explained as follows. King Abgar IX, king of Edessa (today's Urfa

View of the mosaic floor between parts of the wall.

Street front of today's church of St Peter upon Cornhill (after the great fire it was rebuilt by Wren between 1677 and 1687); Cornhill near Gracechurch Street.

Copper nail and green mosaic stone which was imported from Italy; both from the second-century private house, St Bride's, Fleet Street.

in Turkey) was also called Lucius and he also corresponded with Pope Eleutherius after his conversion.

Lucius (Abgar) of Edessa was thus confused with Lucius the Briton, who was subsequently linked with a church.

A brass tablet from the time of Henry IV (1399–1415) which can still be seen in St Peter upon Cornhill tells the story of the church's foundation as if it were a matter of fact (page 77).

The church's existence is attested from 1044, shortly before the Norman Conquest. In 1666 the whole structure was destroyed by the Great Fire of London and was subsequently rebuilt by Sir Christopher Wren, the most eminent architect of the seventeenth century.

The German composer Felix Mendelssohn-Bartholdy played on the church's organ in 1840 and called it the most splendid organ of London, so adding to its fame. There are many reasons, therefore, to come here and meditate on history, legend and reality.

Searching for traces of early Christianity in London is still as difficult as ever. Until now little indisputable evidence has been found. Excavations that are highly desirable, as for example under the church of St Andrew, Holburn, are hardly possibly at this time.

Consequently the historian has to rely on probab-ilities and presumptions. After separating these from obvious legends we

may conclude that Christian communities were active in London at least from the second century onwards just as they were in Gaul and along the river Rhine.

Provincial Christians

There are only scant traces of early Christianity in London. Yet the conclusion that few or no Christians lived in Britain in the early period would be misguided. Especially in the big cities they could live relatively safely, without being recognized if they did not want to be.

Furthermore, Christianity was

mainly a religion of the cities during the first centuries. Only later did it reach smaller villages and countryside areas. The English word 'pagans' for heathen or unbelievers may illustrate this. It is derived etymologically from the term *pagani* meaning 'people from the countryside' or 'from the villages'.

Obviously only a few excavations are possible in densely populated urban areas. This contributes to the small amount of archaeological discoveries in London compared to the finds at Lullingstone, in Kent.

Particularly in Britain there are many smaller settlements outside the main administrative centres where reliable archaeological evidence for Christian settlements has been found. The scholarly debate on the exact dating of such evidence is often characterized by ideological considerations arising from the history of religion.

Many people believe that no Christian seals, Christian churches or other overtly Christian artefacts could have existed prior to Constantine's edict of Milan which legalized Christianity in AD313. Consequently they do not date such discoveries earlier than 313.

A more open-minded approach, however, may allow for an earlier date in some cases. Places like Water Newton (Durobrivae, Cambridgeshire),

St Peter upon Cornhill, its front facing the garden on the site of the ancient Roman basilica. The area is now packed with modern buildings.

Inscription on the brass tablet in the vestry of St Peter upon Cornhill telling the story of how King Lucius founded the church in AD179.

BEE IT KNOWNE TO ALL MEN THAT IN THE YEARE OF OVR LORD GOD 179. *LVCIVS* THE FIRST CHRISTIAN KING OF THIS LAND, THEN CALLED BRITAINE, FOVNDED Ŷ FIRST CHVRCH IN LONDON, THAT IS TO SAY, Ŷ CHVRCH OF S. PETER VPON CORNEHILL : AND HEE FOVNDED THERE AN ARCHBIS = HOP'S SEE, AND MADE THAT CHVRCH Ŷ METROPOLITANE AND CHEIFE CHVRCH OF THIS KINGDOME, AND SO IT INDVRED Ŷ SPACE OF 400 YEARES AND MORE, VNTO THE COMING OF S. AVSTIN THE APOSTLE OF ENGLAND, THE WHICH WAS SENT INTO THIS LAND BY S. GREGORIE, Ŷ DOCTOR OF Ŷ CHVRCH IN THE TIME OF KING ETHELBERT : AND THEN WAS THE ARCH= BISHOP'S SEE & PALL REMOVED FROM Ŷ FORESAID CHVRCH OF S. PETER VPON CORNEHILL VNTO DOROBERNIA, THAT NOW IS CALLED CANTERBVRIE, & THERE IT REMAINETH TO THIS DAY, AND MILLET A MONKE WHICH CAME INTO THIS LAND WITH S. AVSTIN, HEE WAS MADE THE FIRST BISHOP OF LONDON, AND HIS SEE WAS MADE IN PAVL'S CHVRCH, AND THIS *LVCIVS* KING WAS THE FIRST FOVNDER OF S. PETERS CHVRCH VPON CORNEHILL, & HEE REIGNED KING IN THIS LAND AFTER BRVTE 1245, YEARES · AND IN THE YEARE OF OVR LORD GOD 124 · *LVCIVS* WAS CROWNED KING : AND THE YEARES OF HIS REIGNE WERE 77 YEARES · AND HEE WAS BV= RIED (AFTER SOME CHRONICLES) AT LONDON : AND AFTER SOME CHRONICLES HEE WAS BVRIED AT GLOCESTER, IN THAT PLACE WHERE Ŷ ORDER OF S. FRANCIS STANDETH NOW.

Lullingstone (near Eynsford in Kent), Richborough (Rutupiae, Kent), Icklingham (Suffolk), Cirencester (Corinium Dobunnorum, in Gloucestershire), Frampton (Dorset), Hinton St Mary (Dorset) or Stone-by-Faversham (Kent) provide many clues to a confident Christianity which was active both in public and in private. One key example is the church in Silchester (Calleva Atrebatum, Hampshire) with its baptistry. The next chapter deals with the discoveries there.

Silchester and its Church

There is quite a lot of evidence for Christian activities long before the time of the emperor Constantine. Surprisingly perhaps, some of the most impressive sites appear to carry little or no significance in modern Britain. One of them is Silchester, where a wealth of artefacts and buildings have been discovered, including one which may well be the first purpose-built church so far discovered north of the Alps.

Silchester. Christian church after excavation. Today, what was once visible has again been buried and is now under arable farmland.

OPPOSITE: Aerial photograph of the ancient town with the Roman wall, from the west. Only in the area around the basilica do some of the excavations remain visible. To the left ancient streets and the outlines of walls can be detected from the differing heights of grass and corn. At the east end of the wall (upper margin) is the church of St Mary the Virgin with surrounding buildings

Silchester (Calleva Atrebatum). Fourth-century town wall. View of its eastern side with the church of St Mary the Virgin. Remains of a Roman temple have been discovered below the church.

A buried town

Silchester is an example of how not to preserve one's ancient heritage. Although much had been unearthed in excavations the area is now once again covered by soil. Uniquely in England, the exact outlines of a whole Roman town are known from well-preserved parts of the ancient town wall. Even a brief look at the prominent church of St Mary the Virgin (picture below) raises hopes that it may be possible to view the whole development from the church's origins in 1180 until the present time. However, disappointment comes when the area is viewed from a closer perspective. The middle of the older aerial photograph (top of page 81) still shows the vicinity of the basilica, the public administration building. Today, however, only the contours of the different heights of grass and corn allow a guess as to how much could be discovered if it were still possible. Unfortunately, Hampshire County Council decided in favour of crop production over the preservation of this unique heritage of an ancient Roman town. Everything that had been unearthed in several excavations between 1866 and 1962 and everything that still could have been

uncovered is now inaccessible because it is covered with soil: the forum, the basilica, the temples, the large guest house (*mansio*), the public baths, the shops, houses and streets and, last but not least, the church south of the basilica.

Luckily the Historic Buildings and Monuments Commission still preserves the wall and parts of the area outside it. Although it has only restricted financial means this body is able to conduct occasional excavations, as for example the unearthing of the amphitheatre between 1981 and 1982 (second picture page 81). Situated on the eastern edge of the town, it was probably built between AD43 and 70. It could host a maximum of 9000 spectators, which underlines its big influence. Two recesses which originally may have been roofed are still well preserved (the third picture on page 81 shows the western recess). Like other sites, such as Caerleon in Wales (Isca Silurum) it is possible that they contained statues of Nemesis, the goddess of fate. This is quite plausible considering the uncertain fate of the gladiators who fought there. The alternative explanation that it may have been a rest room for the fighters is unlikely considering the small space provided.

In 1975 the southern gate was excavated, and in 1976 and 1991 the south-eastern and the northern gates (picture bottom page 81). The view from the

Southern entrance of the amphitheatre.

Western recess in the amphitheatre, possibly the location of a statue of Nemesis, the goddess of fate.

View from the northern gate across the excavated area which is once again covered by soil.

Seal made of lead with Chi-Rho and omega (the alpha is lost through damage).

northern gate shows the area towards the basilica and the church where Calleva Atrebatum is once again covered with soil.

Wealthy citizens: natives and Romans

Silchester had already been settled in pre-Roman times, and

building activities continued into the fourth century. A first pinnacle was reached with the formation of the road-system, probably during the time of Nero (AD54–68), for a brick stamp with his name NERO[O] CL[AUDIUS] CAE[SAR] AUG[USTUS] GER[MANICUS] on it found here dates from this time (see picture). The public buildings, especially the basilica and the baths, were enlarged and constantly refined. Private houses had mosaic floors. A finely chased golden finger ring with a blue onyx stone found here reveals wealth and good taste. However, the question of the town's status within the system of Roman Britain remains unanswered. Was it a so-called *civitas peregrina*, a town with a majority of native citizens? It may also have been given greater status towards the end of the second century or during the visit of the emperor Septimus Severus in Britain (208–10). The emperor marched north to Scotland and thus needed a reliable support in the south. It may well have been in connection with this that Calleva Atrebatum, which had already proved its loyalty, was made a *municipium* or even an official *civitas* with a local administration. In fact no disturbances or revolts amongst the citizens of the town are attested.

The area of the town was 43 hectares. According to the number of houses which have been identified, the population

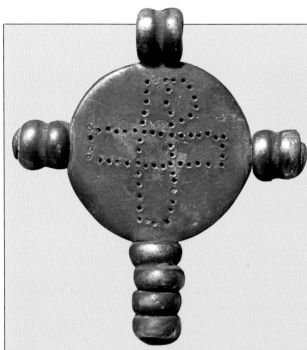

The Monogram of Christ

Christian symbolism was mainly derived from the New Testament. It spread in Britain at an early stage. One of the latest important discoveries in this respect was made in a grave near Shepton Mallet in Somerset in 1990. A silver amulet with a cross was uncovered. It had the two Greek letters Chi-Rho on it, the first letters of the name Christ (picture above to the left, in double size). In 1975 another silver treasure was discovered in Water Newton (Durobrivae). It is the oldest Christian silver treasure found to date in the entire Roman Empire. On several silver triangles the Chi-Rho sign framed by the alpha and omega can be seen. This same symbol signifying beginning and end in Christ can be found on a baptismal font made of lead discovered in Icklingham in Suffolk (picture in the middle and below). With a diametre of about 80cm and a capacity of 175l it was well suited for small baptismal ceremonies in different places. Ten such portable baptismal fonts have been found in Britain so far.

Usually the introduction of this monogram of Christ is traced back to Constantine's vision before the decisive battle against his co-regent Maximus in AD312. Three accounts of this incident exist, two by Constantine's court historian Eusebius and one by his private tutor and philosopher Lactantius. Lactantius gives the shorter and more level-headed description. He writes: 'In his sleep Constantine was admonished to fix the heavenly symbol to the shields (of his soldiers) and to start the battle thus prepared. He did as he was ordered and by bending the top of the letter X (i.e. the Greek Chi) he fixed Christ to the shields.'

The words of Lactantius led to the assumption that Constantine envisaged a real image. Eusebius doesn't mention that the emperor saw this sign for the first time in his vision. Therefore it can be assumed that he derived it from models known to him before. Among the symbols shown here the Chi-Rho monogram from Shepton comes closest to the descriptions of Constantine's sign.

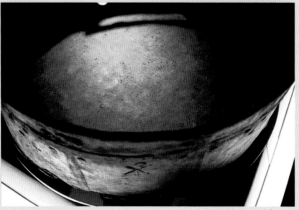

The church of Silchester: the white and black checkered apse mosaic shows an isosceles cross.

was about 2000 people at most. The inhabitants of the suburbs must be added to this number as well, for they had easy access to this business centre through the different town gates (at least five can be identified with certainty). Its role as a marketplace and link on the way to and from the west was secured by a well-established road which linked Silchester with London.

The assumption that the Romans carried out most of the building-work may explain why settlement in Silchester stopped around the middle of the fifth century. When the Roman administration and military withdrew from Britain, Silchester also vanished from history.

The first Christians appear

During excavations near the basilica a seal made of lead was discovered. It is slightly damaged, but a monogram of Christ on it is clearly visible. The monogram shows the intermingled Greek letters Chi and Rho, the first letters of the name of Christ (picture page 83). On the right side of the seal is an omega. Originally an alpha was inscribed opposite it. According to Revelation 1:8 and 22:13 these letters, the first and last in the Greek alphabet, are a sign for beginning and end in Christ— Christ shares God's eternity. It may well be that this seal was in official use, for it was found near a public building. This, however, may have been possible only after 313 when Constantine and Licinius legalized Christianity. Nevertheless, it is also possible that it was used earlier. Constantius Chlorus, the father of Constantine the Great, was the ruler of the Western Empire. He reigned in Britain from 293 until 297 and in the year of his death in 306. Even under his rule

The church of Silchester as it was excavated in 1961. At the bottom of the picture is the baptistry with the brick floor.

Reconstruction of the church of Silchester as it may have looked in the mid-fourth century after the official establishment of Christianity in the Roman Empire. Previous structures appear to have been built with wooden walls on stone foundations.

Christians were tolerated much more than before; recent scholarship confirms that neither he nor his son Constantine who succeeded him in 306 joined in the disastrous persecution of Christians under Diocletian, at the end of the third century. Therefore it is possible that Christian officials may have used such seals here in Britain at least in a church or private context before 313. It was not until later, when this monogram of Christ appeared to Constantine in a vision (see also the reports of Eusebius and Lactantius) before the final battle against Maxentius in 312, that it was used as an official symbol in state affairs and public administration. Consequently it cannot be ruled out that Constantine knew of this symbol through his contacts with high-ranking Christians in Britain.

It is equally difficult to classify the church of Calleva Atrebatum. A building of 13m by 9m was discovered immediately south of the forum. It consists of a portal, a central nave and two side naves and has an apse pointing west. The central nave had a simple red floor which is now almost entirely destroyed. The apse had a white and black

Sketch of the church of Silchester and its baptistry about the end of the third or the beginning of the fourth century.

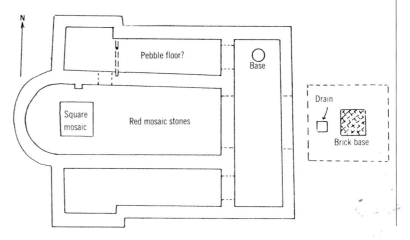

N

Pebble floor?

Base

Square mosaic

Red mosaic stones

Drain

Brick base

THE HERITAGE OF THE FIRST CHRISTIANS

checkered mosaic showing an isosceles (equal-armed) cross (picture page 84). Its small size and the modest Christian symbolism point to an early date (although the details of the altar and wall decorations may have used more symbols). The fact that the apse pointed west instead of east as in later church buildings points to a time when church architecture was not yet formalized.

Another interesting feature is a small area of about 1.2 square metres found 3.5m east of the church's entrance (see sketch bottom page 85). Presumably a portable baptismal font stood here, similar to others found elsewhere in Britain (see caption on page 83). If the assumptions above are correct this also points to an early period when Christianity was still not established as a legal religion in the Roman Empire. It cannot be proved that the church was entirely built of stone, as a modern reconstruction suggests. Rather, particular discoveries suggest that only the foundation walls of public buildings in Silchester were made of stone, while the rest was built of bricks and wood. A detail handed down to us by theologian and historian Lactantius, a teacher at Constantine's court in Trier, may be of interest in this respect. He mentions that on one occasion Constantius gave in to anti-Christian attacks and allowed the destruction of Christian meeting places (*conventicula*). However,

in doing so he only allowed 'walls which could be restored' to be destroyed. This reference suggests that the attacks were directed against public Christian meeting places rather than private houses. It also suggests that Constantius did not allow the complete destruction of these buildings. Rather, he sought a compromise in restricting the destructions to buildings with wooden walls which could easily be restored. Thus a modest mosaic cross like than one in the apse of the church in Silchester and its portable baptismal font may well have escaped the destruction.

In the light of these considerations it is possible that the church of Silchester already existed in the time of Constantius Chlorus, during the late third century. If this is correct it would be the oldest church to have been discovered north of the Alps so far. Indeed, it may be one of the oldest churches, if not the oldest, in the entire Roman Empire built for the purpose of Christian worship.

The Turning Point:
York and Constantine

When Constantine was made emperor by his troops at York, after the death of his father Constantius in 306, Christian optimism rose throughout the western empire. For while Constantius had at best been neutral, Constantine had shown signs of pro-Christian tendencies for some time. Not much of Roman York has been excavated, and this damaged bust of the emperor is one of the few important discoveries from that period.

Bust of Constantine the Great as a young man, found at York, now in York Museum.

Background

By the end of the third century Britain had been well developed by the Romans (see map). Only Scotland was barely penetrable. Instead of being markers of influence in the north, Hadrian's Wall and the Antonine Wall served rather to defend the southern regions against the Scottish population. Nevertheless, a Roman presence in the southern and western areas of Wales and Cornwall can be demonstrated, although there have been no remarkable discoveries there. Just one example of Roman presence is the fact that almost the entire tin trade was carried out in Wales. A milestone of Constantine the Great displayed in the church of St Hilary shows that Roman influence reached even this remote corner.

Two of the earliest traces of Christianization in Britain are found in the east of Wales. Remains in Caerleon (Isca Silurum) and Caerwent (Venta Silurum) may even date back even to the pre-Constantine period. However, the identification and

Map with the most important Roman settlements, road networks and locations of archaeological discoveries in Britain until the fourth century.

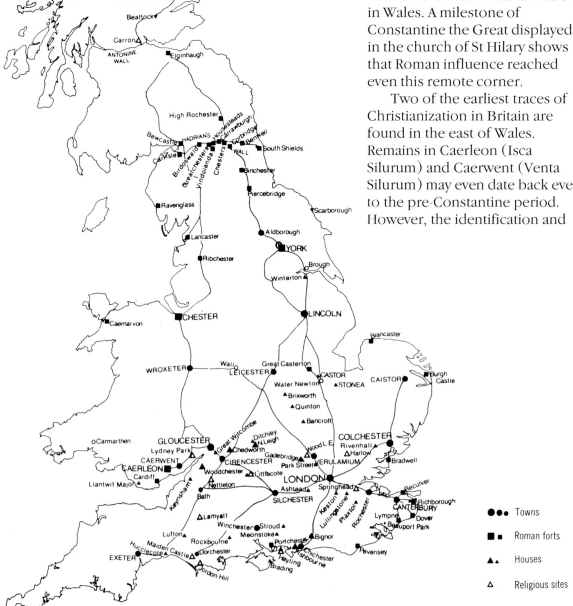

		Towns
■ ■	■	Roman forts
▲ ▲		Houses
△		Religious sites

evaluation of some discoveries in Caerwent like the house church in the so-called 'house XXII north' and the 'shrine of the head' in insula XI are still a matter of dispute. The two martyrs Aaron and Julius probably lived in Caerleon during the persecution under Decius when the second legion of Augustus was stationed here.

There are more such examples which show that Constantine was operating in a well-structured region after he became *Augustus* (another title for Caesar) of the western empire in York in 306. They also show that Christianity was already widespread throughout Britain. York (Eburacum) was raised to the status of *colonia* by the emperor Septimius Severus (193–211). When Britain was divided into *Britannia superior* (the south) and *Britannia inferior* (the

north) it became the capital of the smaller northern area of *Britannia inferior*. It is not clear exactly when this happened but most probably it was some time between AD197 and 216. From then on York enjoyed equal status to London, the capital of the southern region, at least in theory.

Severus was in York in the beginning of 211 and died there on 4 February 211. Afterwards

*W*all painted with frescoes in the office of the *principia* under the present York Minster, early third century AD.

*M*ultangular Tower of the Roman town fortification of York. Foundations from AD70. It was enlarged under Constantius towards the end of the third century. The remains of the city wall are about 5.5m high.

Constantius used York as residence again until 306. He also died there, on 25 July of that year. His son may have felt uncomfortable about reigning from a residence where two of his predecessors had died so soon after their arrival and he stayed for only a short time. Only in autumn 313, some months after the Edict of Milan which legalised Christianity, did he return to Britain and York.

Scant remains

Most remains of archaeological interest in York stem from the time of Constantius. The *Mult-angular Tower* is one of the outstanding monuments. Some of the buildings which preceded the tower even go back to the foundation period of York (page 89 bottom). It owes its name to its ten corners. The walls are about 1.50m thick and about 5.50m high. Originally it may have been much higher. Roman sarcophagi and a Roman sewage channel similar to the installation in Cologne were discovered in the vicinity (see also page 56). It is 46m long and 1.5m high. Although it was discovered in 1972 no further finds have been uncovered there since.

The picture of the Multangular Tower shows the ruins of the fort's wall which was enlarged and significantly improved under Constantius and possibly his son Constantine. These ruins are still 4m high and

11m long, giving a good impression of the fort's strength. The so-called East Corner Tower also belongs to this complex. Its ruins reach a height of only 2.7m. Other ruins of the wall are visible around the ancient Roman site.

As only a few finds were made within the actual town wall it is difficult to describe the town's appearance at the time of the turning-point under Constantine. The inner city is so densely populated that it is difficult to make systematic excavations. Among the few discoveries there is a large bathroom under the Mail Coach Inn near St Sampson's Square. Possibly the most interesting discoveries are below York Minster. During restoration works parts of the *principia*, headquarters of the Roman garrison, were found. Among the discoveries were small objects like theatre masks and figurines, but much more important are the wall paintings in a large office at the back of the complex (page 89). Today they have been carefully restored and are among Britain's most impressive Roman frescoes. The building can be dated to the end of the third century and it is possible that this office was used by Constantius and Constantine.

Father, mother, son and the turning-point in world history

The royal family which helped Christianity to become the

official religion of the empire is very atypical of the common concept of a Roman Caesar's family. Constantius (picture at top of page) was born the son of a common family in Illyricum, the present Dalmatia, on 31 March 250. Even as a young man he was a well-tried soldier and officer and was governor of the province of Dardania (today's Serbia) in Naissa (on the River Nissava). He fell in love with Helena, the owner of a guesthouse (centre picture), but as a high-ranking Roman officer he was not allowed to marry a non-Roman wife. They lived together without being married and had a son called Constantine (bottom picture). The year of his birth is disputed, being either 285, 272 or 273. In Naissa the actual day, 27 February, later became a festival lasting several days.

Constantius had a very successful career. Maximianus, co-regent of Diocletian, appointed him prefect of the Praetorian Guard. He separated from Helena and their common-law son in order to marry Theodora, Maximian's stepdaughter, but although he had children by her, including three sons, he always saw Constantine as his firstborn and heir. Thus he still provided for him and his mother. A concubine and illegitimate children were quite acceptable in Roman society, and even separation from the concubine in order to marry was accepted as long as the 'divorced' was provided for. As

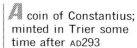

A coin of Constantius; minted in Trier some time after AD293

A coin of Helena; struck in her memory by her grandson Constantius II in Constantinople (Byzantium) in the year of her death, AD329.

A coin of Constantine the Great, minted at Siscia in Pannonia (the modern Sisak in Hungary). Constantine looks very young on the picture, and it may have been struck immediately after 314 when he became head of the provinces along the River Danube as well.

Milestone of Maximian, Augustus of the western empire until 305, and his 'sub—emperor', Constantius. The stone was erected between 293 and 305 when Constantius had his residence mainly in Trier. It was placed along the road from Trier to Cologne, just 2200m outside the western gate of Roman Cologne. NOBILISSIMIS CAESARIBUS CO(N)STANTINO ET MAXI- MINIAN(O) INVICTIS A C(OLONIA) A(GRIPPINENSIUM) L(EUGA) I = 'To the noble emperors Constantius and Maximian, invincible. From Cologne 1 League.' (One league is 2200m.) With the help of this milestone the administrative system after Diocletian's reform can be explained. There were two main emperors (*Augusti*), one for the western empire (Maximian) and one for the eastern empire (Diocletian, who as first among equals ensured his influence in the western part). Each of them had a 'sub-emperor'. Diocletian chose Galerius while Maximian chose Constantius who succeeded him in 305. Both of them appear together on the milestone from Cologne.

far as we know, Helena and Constantine remained near him, and when Maximian made him Caesar of Gaul and Britain he took both of them with him to his capital and residence Trier (see milestone left). From there Constantine was sent to the court of the emperor Diocletian in Nicomedia, the capital of Bithynia. While he was with the emperor he received a comprehensive military and intellectual education, and met the orator and philosopher Lactantius who confessed his Christian faith immediately before the persecution under Diocletian in 303. He survived, and in 317 he was appointed teacher to Constantine's own son in Trier.

It has been assumed that Helena was a Jewess or at least a 'God-fearing' person close to Judaism before she became a Christian. This remains a matter of speculation. The claim that Constantine's stepmother Theodora was Christian has more credibility. This can be argued from the fact that she risked calling her second daughter Anastasia, which means 'resurrection', even shortly before the major persecution of Christians under Diocletian. This would hardly have been possible without the consent of her husband.

Against this background Constantius' sometimes friendly, tolerant behaviour towards Christians, and some of his compromises, can be understood. It is obvious that Constantine was influenced by the tolerant, and sometimes even pro-Christian, attitude of his father and stepmother.

When his father died, aged fifty-six, on 25 July 306, Constantine was with him. Immediately his troops announced him as his father's successor although the latter had been Augustus of the whole western empire for only a year.

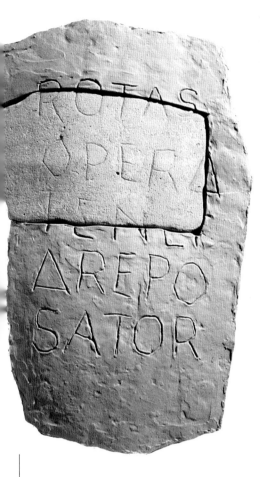

A time of transition: ambiguous symbolism

Constantius and Constantine lived in a transitary period between Roman polytheism, monotheism and Christianity. This gave rise to ambiguous expressions, texts and inscriptions. The 'SATOR' square found in different parts of the Roman empire is a very famous example of this. (Amongst other places where it was found, Pompeii is noteworthy because the writing must have predated the town's destruction by

Vesuvius in AD79!) Two examples have been found in Britain. One palindrome from Cirencester (Corinium Dobunnorum) was scratched on wall plaster (bottom right). A second was found on a rubbish heap at the ancient Roman garrison in Manchester (Mamucium). The fragmentary text was written on a broken piece of an amphora. It contains the following words:

R	O	T	A	S
O	P	E	R	A
T	E	N	E	T
A	R	E	P	O
S	A	T	O	R

Word for word, this translates as: 'The wheels / carefully / holds / Arepo / the sower.' It functions as a palindrome, the letters forming the same expression no matter which way they are read. Part of the ambiguity lies in the word *Sator* which not only means 'sower' but also 'creator'. Readers with a Christian background understood the allusion to God. The impression is reinforced by the fact that the proper name Arepo starts with an A and ends in an O, the combination representing the 'alpha and omega', the beginning and end in Christ. In addition, a rearrangement of the letters produces the beginning of the

'S ATOR'— A palindrome (phrase reading the same backwards as forward) from Manchester, on a broken piece of an amphora—wine storage jar—from the end of the second century. It must remain open whether the text was part of the amphora's original decoration or whether it was scratched later on one of the broken pieces.

'S ATOR'— A palindrome from Cirencester, engraved on wall plaster found after it had fallen down; end of second century AD.

93

Latin version of the Lord's Prayer, again framed by the symbols A and O:

```
                      P
                      A
          A     T     O
                      E
                      R
P A T E R N O S T E R
                      O
                      S
          A     T     O
                      E
                      R
```

The palindromes from Cirencester (discovered in 1868) and Manchester (discovered in 1978) are both dated to the second century AD. There is no clear archaeological evidence for Christian influence in Cirencester and Manchester during that time. By contrast, the Christian interpretation of the palindrome from Pompeii (prior to AD79) is supported by other evidence as well (see above), in spite of contradictory hypotheses that are still current.

However, it is not necessary to use the 'Paternoster' pattern in order to find a Christian symbol in these palindromes. Even in their present form without any rearrangement the words 'TENET' read horizontally and vertically build an isosceles cross

transmitting the information: 'HE (the creator/Christ) HOLDS'.

In AD165 the Latin apologist Minutius Felix quotes a non-Christian as stating that Christians recognize each other because of 'secret symbols and signs' (*occultis se notis et insignibus noscunt*). About three decades later Tertullian writes about Christians honouring the cross and different forms of its representation. Consequently such palindromes may have been in use long before the time of Constantine. Their ambiguity was especially important before his time, when being an open Christian was unsafe.

Treasure of a Changing Society

Scarce though the archaeological evidence for pre-Christian art in Britain may be, the finds of the Constantinian period are many and fascinating. Fourth-century British Christianity was at the forefront of art and inventiveness even in the non-Christian society which preceded and accompanied it, and Christians no longer hesitated to decorate their houses and household goods openly with symbols and inscriptions. At Lullingstone, one wall painting in an extensive villa shows several people in the position of prayer characteristic of the period.

Lullingstone; 'Orans' (man at prayer), partly reconstructed, now in the British Museum, London.

A villa near the riverside

Even in Roman times, living in the countryside was considered a privilege and some Romans chose to live in one of the most beautiful corners of the modern county of Kent. They lived in Lullingstone, just west of Eynsford, in a villa along the river Darenth.

The Anglo-Saxons knew that an important structure must have stood in the area before its complete destruction by fire in the fifth century, for they built a church here in the seventh century.

In the eighteenth century memory of this Roman villa had still not faded, but it was not until 1949 that systematic excavations began (see picture page 98 top). After twelve years of excavation work the picture became clear. As early as about AD60 a villa was built here.

Its owners changed repeatedly and it was constantly being enlarged and embellished. Finally, in the fourth century, it belonged to a Christian family who installed a fine chapel in the building. While there is only circumstantial evidence for Christian houses in London, the evidence here is beyond doubt.

Although the paintings of people at prayer (see picture page 98 middle) may have been made by non-Christians the big 'Chi-Rho' with the alpha and omega clearly indicates a Christian background. However, it is difficult to reach any conclusion about the place of these discoveries in Lullingstone's history.

The oldest house was built in stone during the time of Nero and had a special feature—a room built much deeper into the floor than the rest of the building. From the west of the house it could be reached via stairs, and a ramp led into it from the house's entrance.

During this first phase it probably served as a cool cellar for grain and wine. The style of the house is a smaller variant of the villa von Wittlich. The architecture of both buildings was determined by the sloping ground on which they were built.

Towards the end of the second century the house had a new owner who made a lot of changes. A bathroom was installed, and adjoining houses and a well were built. Most significant, however, is the fact that the cellar became a cult chamber. Now there was a wall-painting with three nymphs in one of the niches. In the centre of the room a pool was installed and filled with water.

It is very tempting to assume that this was a baptistry, and that the picture of the three nymphs was older so the two features were found together only by accident. Nevertheless, this is not very likely when seen in context, for there was a cult of nymphs connected with such pools. The cult of water nymphs was probably an obvious option for pre-Christian Romans living here,

*T*he villa of Lullingstone in its present condition. At the top is the floor mosaic; the room with Christian features is off the picture to the right.

near a river and close to the water level.

When the first Christians moved to Lullingstone they must have appreciated this favourable location as they built the room for their services directly above this cult cellar, and it cannot be ruled out that they actually used the 'nymph pool' as a baptistry.

*T*he *Orantes* (people at prayer) from Lullingstone after restoration.

*T*he monogram of Christ, the Chi-Rho, from Lullingstone after restoration. The skilful design imparts a special solemnity to this Christian symbol.

OPPOSITE: Silver vessel from the treasure discovered at Water Newton. Between the first word of the dedicatory inscription (INNOCENTIA) and the partly preserved last word (...RUNT) is the Chi-Rho monogram with alpha and omega.

The silver treasure (28 objects) of Water Newton (Durobrivae), today in the British Museum, London.

The silver vessel of Publianus from the treasure of Water Newton. Again, it has the monogram of Christ with alpha and omega, written between the last word of the text at the left (HONORO) and the first word at the right (SANCTUM). The owner's name is written at the bottom of the vessel.

This would fit in well with the strategy of substituting Christian values for old customs; it is clear that Christian cult and symbols often took the place of old pagan cults and symbols without necessarily destroying them. As a matter of fact pictures with scenes from Greek myths were preserved in other rooms of the villa as well, even during a phase when big Christian wall-paintings were drawn there.

Although the building was not occupied for some time during the third century, significant changes were made shortly before the turn of the century. The cult chamber seems now to have been used for different rites. Two older busts placed there suggest that it was a kind of ancestor cult.

Most significant is the fact that the central room was now furnished with a fine floor mosaic. One of its central scenes is Europa being kidnapped by Zeus (Jupiter) in the form of a white bull. It is accompanied by a Latin couplet reminiscent of Ovid's *Metamorphoses*—art and literature went hand in hand in a very natural way. In contrast to today, this was a matter of course in Christian circles as well.

Another example of this is the chest of Proiecta from the Esquiline in Rome (see margin page 100). During this generation, by AD330 at the latest (hardly as late as the end of the century, as some scholars still maintain), it is possible to find Christians and followers of the older religions living together without complications, at least in Lullingstone.

This may be deduced from the fact that the rooms decorated with pagan features were used unchanged and undamaged until the fifth century while at the same time the rooms just above and next to the old cult chamber were furnished with Christian frescoes. These are the oldest frescoes north of the Alps in living-rooms which can clearly be identified as such.

However, these frescoes also transmit a clear message. The big Chi-Rho symbol in the anteroom to the actual chapel was deliberately made bigger than the old frescoes with the nymphs in the *Nymphaeum* below. It asserted the superiority of Christianity.

The people at prayer in the chapel were pictured with details of their faces. They were mourning for a dead person. The dead person, surrounded by mourners, was also portrayed in a praying position and was identified by a stylized curtain which symbolized death. This

scene demonstrated that the old ancestor cult displayed in the ancient *Nymphaeum* no longer had any function.

Christians mourning for their dead in prayer know that beginning and end, as well as resurrection, are a reality in Christ, not in bygone mythical ideologies. The artefacts in the Lullingstone villa display this in a subtle and impressive way.

Treasures in the soil

A sensational discovery was made in 1975. No other find of the period worldwide is as significant as this. A silver treasure consisting of several pieces (see picture above) was discovered in Water Newton, the Roman Durobrivae.

It is special not only because of the number of objects and their value, but also because it belongs to the early Constantinian period (top of

*T*hree silver sheets from the Water Newton treasure. Similar to pre-Christian votive plaques, thin pieces like these were fixed to walls and portable objects. In Christian contexts they were also fixed to altars. One particular piece (not shown here) carries the inscription IAMCILLA VOTUM QUOD PROMI-SIT CON- PLEVIT, 'Iam-cilla has fulfilled the vow she promised'. Similar inscriptions were also used on non-Christian votive plaques. Their Christian origin can only be proved by the mono-gram of Christ. From such votive pieces we know the names of four people from the Christian community in Durobrivae: Publianus and the three women Innocentia, Viventia and Iamcilla.

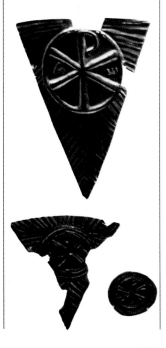

A bride's chest from the silver treasure of Proiecta. It was found on the Esquiline hill in Rome in 1793 and also displays Christian and non-Christ-ian motifs used together by a family in the second half of the fourth century. Below the couple, Secundus and Proiecta, is a scene of Venus dressing herself, a popular mythical scene. However, the text below reads: SECUNDUS ET PROIECTA, VIVATIS IN CHRISTU, 'Secundus and Proiecta, may you live in Christ'.

In a Roman dwelling house of the second to fourth centuries, beneath the Roman church of SS Giovanni e Paolo, frescoes with praying Christians were found near to a picture of Venus.

picture on page 98). Nothing comparable has been discovered at any other site in the Roman Empire . Only the so-called SEVSO treasure from Roman Pannonia (which today is distributed between Hungary and the former Yugoslavia) may become similarly important. It made headlines at the beginning of 1990. The artistic and material value of this treasure may be even higher but its dates are significantly later, towards the end of the fourth century.

One thing both treasures have in common is that they were not found by archaeologists. (The treasure in Water Newton was discovered with a metal detector.) Therefore nobody knows the exact location where they were kept, hidden or left behind, and so far we know nothing of the finer details of the Christians in Water Newton or of Seuso (modern transliteration) and their social and topographic circumstances.

A further complication concerning Water Newton is the fact that the Roman settlement of Durobrivae has not yet been excavated. Like Silchester, an aerial view shows the outline of the site and the course of the wall around an area of about 18 hectares and a Roman camp. Nevertheless, the excavation work itself remains to be done.

Nobody knows whether, in the future, traces of an early Christian church similar to Silchester will be found. What we know is that this town was built in a very fertile region near Peterborough in Cambridgeshire. This circumstance may have helped its inhabitants to become extraordinarily rich.

In addition, it was the only town in an archaeologically confirmed centre for ceramics trading and iron works. The road link between London in the south and Lincoln (Lindum) and York (Eburacum) further north was ideal. Furthermore, there was the navigable river Nene just north of the town.

Christians in Durobrivae seem to have profited from its agricultural and industrial wealth. The silver treasure with its nine vessels and nineteen Christain symbols and plaques shows that the church must have been rich. It could afford to show that 'pagans' were not the only well-to-do people.

The finds in Durobrivae (and in Seuso) even give the names of individual Christians. On the bottom of the biggest vessel (picture page 98) is the name of Publianus. Round the rim it bears the inscription SANCTUM ALTARE TUUM DOMINE SUBNIXUS HONORO. The picture clearly shows the Chi-Rho framed by alpha and omega between the words HONORO and SANCTUM. On the other side of the same vessel this symbol is between the letters D and OMINE, because of the layout of the design. A rough translation of the text reads: 'I, being dependent on you, Lord, honour your altar'.

Although it would be stretching the evidence to assume with some interpreters that the word 'altar' actually means 'church' in this context (a part signifying the whole) it is clear from the word that a Christian church room existed here.

The whole treasure with its drinking vessels and wine vessels may indeed have belonged to the dishes used by the church for Holy Communion. A smaller vessel has the inscription INNOCENTIA ET VIVENTIA ...RUNT (top of picture page 99) round its rim. Again there is a Chi-Rho framed by alpha and omega between the letters RUNT and INNOCENTIA. The text mentions two women called Innocentia and Viventia. What they did is unknown to us, for the beginning of the verb form '...runt' has been lost. It is certainly a votive inscription.

A Jewish discovery?

Other single objects found in different places point to a Christian presence as well. One of them is the silver spoon found in Mildenhall (Cunetio) with the monogram of Christ.

However, in this case something very unexpected arises. Here, in Mildenhall, Suffolk, several other precious bowls and vessels were found in 1941, amongst them was a very costly silver bowl with the star of

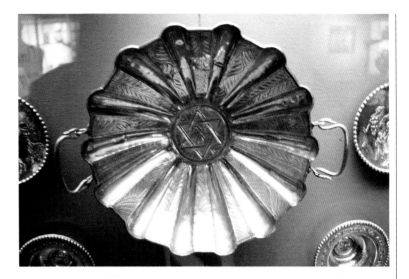

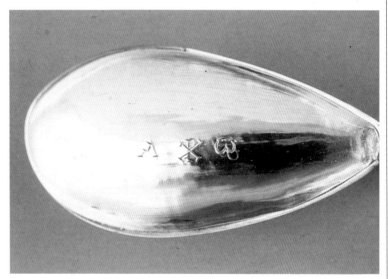

David in the middle (picture page 101).

There is common agreement about the extraordinary wealth of the owner of this treasure. Nonetheless, how is it possible that scenes with pagan mythology (for example, the god Okeanos in the centre of the biggest silver plate), Christian symbols (the Chi-Rho spoons) and the apparently Jewish star of David were found together in

The silver bowl from the treasure of Mildenhall with what seemed to be a Jewish star.

Spoon from the treasure of Mildenhall with the Christian Chi-Rho symbol.

The floor mosaic in Hinton St Mary. Behind Christ's head is the Chi–Rho sign representing the first two letters of the Greek word CHRISTOS. Left and right are two pomegranates, allegorical allusions to the Song of Songs.

one collection?

As we have seen before, there are many comparable examples of Christian and pagan symbols co-existing. However, the star of David is unusual. Its appearance in this context can teach us a lesson on the danger of transferring modern symbolism back into antiquity.

Neither in the fourth century nor shortly before and afterwards was this hexagram (two combined triangles) typical of Judaism. It is true that the symbol is found on the seal of Josua Ben Assajahu dating from the seventh century and on the frieze of the newly built synagogue in Capernaum (fourth or fifth century AD), as well as in many other Jewish contexts.

However, there is no claim whatsoever in all the literature of the period that this symbol had particularly Jewish religious significance. (In contrast the Christian alpha and omega and Chi-Rho have their origin in the religious texts of the New Testament.) Only from the sixth century onwards do literary clues for a clear connection of the hexagram with Jewish faith appear. In its earliest appearances it is not called the star of David but the 'Seal of Solomon'.

Even after this period it more often appears as part of the decoration of Christian churches than in synagogues. It was not until the foundation of the state of Israel in 1949 that the 'Star of David' is mentioned in clearly Jewish contexts. Consequently, the star of David in the treasure of Mildenhall could be a decoration used by a Christian or even a 'pagan' rather than by a Jew, though this cannot be proved.

It is also possible that the treasure belonged to a secularized Jewish family using Greek mythology, which later converted to Christianity. However, in the light of the social circumstances of this period this is not very likely. As in the previous examples, this may be another incident where a Christian did not destroy the earlier non-Christian objects in his possession. Thus it is not necessarily an example of syncretism.

Kenneth Painter, the scholar who published details of the treasure, believes it belonged to the Christian general Lupicinus active in Britain under and partly against Emperor Julian the Apostate (AD360); this must remain an attractive but unconfirmed hypothesis.

The interpretation of the mosaic of Christ in Hinton St Mary in Dorset (picture page 102) appears to be easier. It is 6m by 9m square. Extensive research on it has been done since 1964. Although doubts about its Christian interpretation have been raised occasionally, scholarly consensus has been reached on the picture itself: it is the oldest mosaic representation of Christ in European art. We do not know much about the house to which it belonged.

It seems that shortly after the turning-point under Constantine, Christians responded to the challenge of non-Christian mythology (and its expression in art) in a new way. They represented Christ on a floor mosaic, just as other mosaics used to portray the Olympian gods. In the same way as they were represented on the floor so that people could walk on them, it was no problem to picture Christ on the floor. He who made the old gods obsolete now also took their place in mosaics.

It may be that in designing the mosaic the artists were conscious of the human nature of Christ who humbled himself, the Son of man who fell to the floor under the wooden cross. The fact that he is pictured in Roman style as a beardless young hero adds a special nuance to the picture.

In the corners of the mosaic are four heads which probably represent the four evangelists. The depiction of Bellerophon killing the Chimara is a reinterpretation of old mythology: good defeating evil.

At the same time other

mosaics were laid in Frampton (Dorset), where stylistic evidence points to the same artist), Fifehead Neville (Dorset), Littlecote (Wiltshire) and Pitney (Somerset), which are identifiable as Christian by the Chi-Rho sign and other symbols. Nevertheless, the mosaic of Hinton St Mary surpasses them all as an important witness to a period of change.

Back to the Continent:
Trier and Cologne under Constantine and after

Constantine's architectural activities on the continent, soon after he took up his imperial seat at Trier, were phenomenal. Some of the most fascinating examples have been discovered comparatively recently. The painting on a ceiling at his imperial palace in Trier—which later became part of the huge Christian cathedral—is particularly intriguing.

Portrait of a philosopher, one of the squares in the ceiling at Constantine's palace. Usually interpreted as being a portrait of Lactantius, the Christian historian and theologian who was employed by Constantine as tutor to his family.

Power must be displayed

Constantine's father Constantius had already started systematic building projects in Trier in AD305 and Constantine followed his example in further developing the city. The audience hall was designed to surpass any building in Rome. The construction of the palace-like basilica took six years (see pictures). This showpiece building was 74m long (including the apse) and 32.5m wide. Significantly, it replaced a similar hall (53m by 25m) which his rival Galerius erected at Thessalonica at the same time. For Constantine this was important because Galerius had been the Augustus in the eastern empire since 305 and when the latter chose Thessalonica as his capital it became an immediate rival to the western capital of Trier. As relationships between the two halves of the Roman Empire were not always smooth such achievements had their effect on foreign policy and home affairs.

In 311, however, Galerius did better than Constantine. It was Galerius in Thessalonica who first introduced an official edict which tolerated Christianity, not Constantine, although the latter had been known for his positive attitude towards Christianity for a long time. It was not until two years later that the more famous edict of Milan was introduced by Constantine and Licinius, for the western empire. Even individual formulations in this edict show borrowing from Galerius's version.

Constantine's basilica was not just impressive from the outside. Inside it had all the luxury an emperor in the cool

Interior of Constantine's basilica in Trier; today in use as a Protestant Lutheran church.

north would expect. The hall was more than 2,400m square and had an under-floor heating system. This system was provided with separate units beneath the floor and in the walls so that different sections of the hall could be heated separately. This had the interesting effect that in winter Constantine's guests would have to walk 50m in a cold room before they could appreciate the warmth in which he received them.

On the outside the ancient walls were not much more decorated than they appear today. They were faced with brick and the areas around the windows were decorated with small ornaments. But the interior was much more splendid than the present church. (Since 1856 the basilica has been used as a church (page 106.) The walls were covered with slabs of marble. The holes for the wall plugs which held these slabs are still visible up to the height of the upper window-level. Some of the slabs were covered with colourful motifs. The floor was also made of marble.

A view of the basilica from the park with the seventeenth-century bishop's palace in the foreground gives an impression of its size. The fact that it was not designed as a whole palace but only as a 'simple' audience hall makes its size all the more impressive. Today's remains and what was restored after damage during the war still contain surprises. There were adjoining

North side of Constantine's basilica. The walls have lost their plaster.

buildings, some of which were quite spacious. In 1985 and 1986 remains of the floor of a hall decorated with a mosaic was discovered. Together with a bathroom, parts of which were found nearby, it may have have been part of the palace. In 1983 and 1984 ancient openings or doors were discovered. Presumably they led to private

View of the bishop's palace and Constantine's basilica from the west. Just left of the basilica is one of the towers of the building which now contains two churches Liebfrauen/Cathedral).

rooms for the emperor and to other offices. Constantine's family had another palace near the site where he erected the first church in Trier. Still in the fourth century, it developed into a large double church complex (see model). The view across the park shows how close the two buildings were; the tower of the church is visible between the trees just left of the basilica (see page 107).

Constantine's first church

Originally first-century dwellings and shops stood on the site of the present Liebfrauenkirche and the adjoining cathedral. In the fourth century extensive renovation and building activities started here. The ceiling painting already mentioned was painted in one of the new rooms built. It had dimensions of 10m by 7m. The legend that the house of Constantine's mother, Helena, stood here originated in the ninth century when knowledge of this painting had been lost. This legend asserts that Helena herself had it converted into a church—the present cathedral.

In fact, the ceiling painting was discovered below the present cathedral, and perhaps this does confirm the claim of the *Vita Helenae* (biography of Helena) which was written 500 years later. It is also correct that the northern part of the cathedral shows the walls of the church from the time of Helena and Constantine (picture to the right). Parts of those old walls are

View from the south-east of the model of the double church in the fourth century. To the right is the building which preceded the present cathedral, to the left is the one which preceded the *Liebfrauenkirche*.

coloured pieces of plaster was the impression of a wooden frame which had held the painted plaster in its place. Its pattern helped restorers to put the numerous pieces in their proper places. This technique is still being used; the pattern of the wooden frame is so distinctive that a minute piece can be slotted in simply by looking at the impression on its reverse (see picture on left of page 110). Only afterwards is the result checked from the painted side.

The work of the restorers, Welter and Steffny, together with their team and the excavators,

The north-east front of the modern cathedral looking towards the northern wall of Constantine's time.

up to 25m high. However, the real history of this building belongs to the still unresolved enigmas of the court of the first Christian emperor. This is mainly because more questions than answers about the building were raised when thousands of fragments of fresco paintings were found just a few metres in front of the apse.

Even today not all these fragments have been put together, and new pieces are still being discovered. A special laboratory in the Bishop's Museum is devoted to it (picture on left of page 110). After missing parts had been discovered in 1967 and 1968, a team of restorers worked for fifteen years to put together enough of the ceiling paintings to be able to exhibit them. In the mortar on the back of the

ranks among the most remarkable achievements of modern archaeology. It led to an astonishing discovery: the magnificent ceiling painting with its fifteen different patterns was knocked down only a few years after its creation. A few years later the area around the hall was developed into a big church

Part of the cathedral's northern wall from Constantine's time.

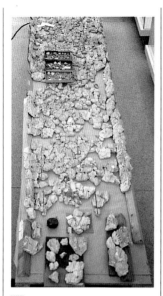

The laboratory where the remains of ceiling and wall paintings from the Constantinian double church are reconstructed.

The picture above right may be a portrait of Helena, the bottom one a portrait of Fausta. Both come from the ceiling painting in the ancient Constantinian house in the cathedral area. The golden nimbus behind their heads origin-ated in pre-Christian portraiture. It was used to highlight rulers or deities. Only later in the development of Christian art did it become the 'halo' designating saints.

which has since become the cathedral. The most satisfying explanation for these circumstances is as follows.

In 321 Crispus, Constantine's oldest son, married. He was the child of Minervina, with whom Constantine had a relationship without being married. This may have been the reason for decorating the palace with the portraits of prominent individuals of the court. However, in 326 Constantine had his son executed, probably charged with adultery with Constantine's wife Fausta (according to the somewhat ambiguous historical sources). Shortly afterwards Constantine also ordered Fausta's execution and she was suffocated in a bath. Afterwards an edict was issued which made both stepmother and son persons who could not be talked about, and any reminder of them in the form of pictures and inscriptions was destroyed. It is likely that in the course of these actions the ceiling painting was demolished as well.

Theodor Kempf discovered the fragments of the painting in 1945. He now believes that the emperor's mother Helena, a very devout Christian, had the church built in place of the palace to atone for her son's cruel (though legal) deed. It may have been her palace, and it was under this church's floor, dating from that time, that the painting was found.

However, the identity of the persons portrayed is not certain.

The philosopher (see page 105) is widely identified with Lactantius. Nevertheless, is the lady highlighted by her position in the centre of the portraits really Constantine's mother Helena (see picture)? Is the young woman with the mirror really Fausta, by whom Constantine had five children and whom he executed in 326? Do the other portraits represent Constantine's sister Constantia, who had been married to his co-regent Licinius since 313, and Crispus' wife Helena? It is possible, but it cannot yet be proved. It must be hoped that the continuing restoration of the wall paintings will provide more evidence in the future.

A sun from Cologne

The tragic activities in Constantine's home undermined his reputation precisely when he consciously wanted to behave as a Christian. In the preceding year the council of Nicaea had taken place (20 May—19 June 325). It was a tactical masterpiece on the part of Constantine to bring to an official end the controversy between two powerful groups, the Arians (who believed that Jesus was only *similar* to God) and the Orthodox (who saw him as *equal* with God). He took a significant part in the formulation of the Nicene Creed, which stated Christ's equality with God and is still used by churches today. The moral shortcomings in his own family so soon afterwards must have come as a shock to him. These circumstances as well as Helena's desire for atonement may have contributed to the architectural expression of the theological emphasis which began in Nicaea.

The awareness of the fallibility of human beings, even Christians, is expressed in contemporary art as well. A typical example of this is a precious cut-glass bowl of this era. It shows Adam and Eve under the tree in Eden, the scene depicting the first case of human disobedience to God (see picture).

In later centuries another church in Cologne was connected with the court in Trier and also with the emperor's

mother Helena. Although this connection can now be shown to be legendary, the church itself still offers very interesting insights. It is the church of St Gereon. Since the Middle Ages it has also been called *ad aureos sanctos*, 'to the golden saints' (see page 112). From the first century AD there had been a cemetery north-west of the Roman town. In the fourth century an oval church was built there. In style it was similar to memorial churches and chapels found elsewhere in the Roman Empire. The interesting questions are: when exactly was it erected, and for whom? Helena died in 329.

Much later, about 590, the Frankish historian Gregory of Tours indicates that the 'golden saints' mentioned in the name

*C*ut-glass bowl with Adam and Eve under the tree in Eden; Cologne, first part of fourth century.

St Gereon, Cologne; view of the apse and the towers.

were the martyrs of the Thebaite Legion which was stationed in Cologne. Some of its soldiers and officers were killed shortly before 269 because of insubordination, possibly during the persecution under Decius. It is said that as a result fifty members of this legion were executed on the order of Maximinian. Although the name Gereon, given to the leader of those troops in Cologne, appears only much later, it is possible that Helena heard about the incident immediately afterwards, for, wherever she was, she (and her son) had immediate access to

Northern wall of St Gereon; remains of the site's earliest period, with a sun made of red brick.

first-hand information, be it in Trier, or, for a certain period of time, at Diocletian's court in Bithynia. There is no evidence for the story that their bodies were thrown into a well and that the memorial church was later erected above it; despite many efforts to trace it, the well has not been found. Nevertheless, the architecture of the church is that of a typical memorial building. The building thus remains a mystery.

However, one answer to the questions mentioned above has now been found. Since 1949, when renovation work at the church was begun after serious damage during the war, traces of the original building have been discovered. Among these were the gold-coloured mosaic stones to which the church owns its 'golden' epithet. The most important discovery, though, was an altar stone to the goddess Isis (picture page 113) discovered in the foundation of the north-west pillar by archaeologist Armin von Gerkan. The damaged inscription on can be reconstructed: ISIDI/MYRIO/ NYMO/...TIUS/...US/ (EX)VOTO/SUSCEPTO/ S(OLVIT) L(IBENS) M(ERITO) L(OCO) D(ATO) D(ECURIONUM) D(ECRETO). In English this says: 'For Isis with the thousand names ...ius ...us has fulfilled his vows gratefully. The town council provides the place (for the altar).'

At first sight this does not seem very exciting. The phenomenon of Christians integrating elements of pagan cult places into their churches, partly to demonstrate Christian superiority, was nothing new in the fourth century. Only the fact that victory over Isis is shown

here is interesting, for she and her son Horus were often (falsely) interpreted as a pre-Christian counterpart to Mary and Jesus. However, the most important fact about this discovery is a coin found in one of the plug holes at the top of the Isis stone. It was a coin of Emperor Constans, a son of Constantine the Great, minted in Trier. He received command over Gaul (with Trier) in April 340. This implies that the coin could not have been put, or have fallen into, this hole prior to that date. As this Isis stone was sealed into the foundation pillar of the building, it is clear that the whole church was not built before 340. This date is clearly too late to attribute the building to Helena.

*D*edication stone of the goddess Isis (for the inscription on it see main text). The coin of Constans minted in Trier in 340 was found in a hole in the top of it.

The exterior of the building poses a further riddle. In the remains of the original northern wall was found a pattern made of brick. It looks like a sun (pictures page 112). Can this be the reply to another challenge to Christianity? Constantine had been accused of worshipping the sun god, the *Sol Invictus* (see pages 125–127). This sign outside a church wall and visible to everybody may be a reply. God is the true sun, and Christ is in God.

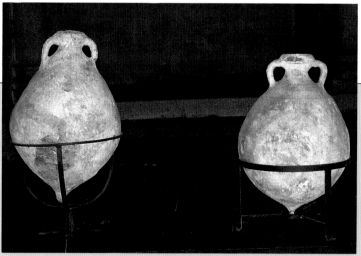

picture). It was erected in 329 along the *Via Labicana*. Colloquially it is still called *'Pignatarra'* gate after the *pignattes*, the amphoras which were built into the vault.

In the course of restoration work amphoras used to strengthen the vault of St Gereon were discovered. These amphoras were about 70cm high and 45cm wide. They were cemented into the walls so as to fill space within the walls without making them too heavy. This was an intelligent way of reducing the weight of the structure. Four of these amphoras are displayed in the church's crypt (see picture). The same technique was used in Helena's mausoleum in Rome (see righthand

An Edict and its Locality:
Milan, around 313

After his conquest of Rome in 312, Constantine met his co-emperor Licinius at Milan in 313 to draft the famous 'edict of Milan' in favour of Christianity. The city was an obvious choice, since it was one of the official capitals of the Roman Empire between 286 and 402. There is little to show for this in Milan today. The derelict remains of the imperial palace, accessible from a side street next to unattractive apartment blocks, give no hint of the importance of the events which took place there.

Walls of a wing of the imperial palace in
Milan, Via Brisa.

Traces of a palace

At the end of the fourth century a certain Ambrose wrote a letter to his sister in which he mentions that twice a day he passes the *regia palatii* near the cemetery *ad Martyres*. The historical and topographical information given by Ambrose has credibility. Aurelius Ambrosius was born in Trier in AD333. From about 374 he was *consularis*, governor of the provinces Liguria and Aemilia. His residence was in Milan. When he tried to negotiate in the controversy about the bishop's successor he himself was made bishop, although at the time he had not even been baptized.

Even though Ambrose hesitated to accept the bishop's office at first, he later developed it into one of the most influential positions in the empire. As adviser he was close to the emperor and also supported him in opposing Gratian, Valentinian II and Theodosius I. It is to him that we owe the oldest evidence about the existence and location of the palace in which the edict of Milan originated. Several sample investigations and surveys since 1943 led to the demarcation of a large area including some buildings. It is located in the western part of the ancient Roman city and, like other Roman residences, near the city wall. The interpretation of the ruins at

The emperor's palace (*regia palatii*) in Milan; remains in the Via Brisa, with a view of what is supposed to be a thermal spa.

the Via Brisa (pictures on pages 115–17) is still controversial. One part has a circular area open on one side (picture page 115–17). Ruins of an apse, rectangular walls and pillars are also visible. Archaeologists in Milan agree that these parts were showpieces of the palace. Its central part may have been a semicircular *Exedra*, a pavilion. In this case it was roofed and had an opening to the south. Adjacent to it was a thermal spa. It is similar to the *Exedra* of the *Domus Augusta*, the palace of the Augustus on the Palatine hill in Rome. It is possible that the edict of Milan was agreed upon nearby.

The so-called 'edict' of Milan is not an actual edict but rather an understanding between the two emperors, allowing Christians not only to worship as they wished, but to receive compensation and return of confiscated property. It exists in two versions which Licinius had sent to the eastern part of the empire. Lactantius hands them down to us as a letter to the governor of Bithynia resident in Nicomedia. (It was publicly announced on 13 June 313.) Eusebius preserves a version which presumably was part of a letter to the governor of Palestine in Caesarea Maritima who held a position similar to Pontius Pilate. In connection with a big exhibition about Milan as a capital of the Roman Empire, further excavations were announced in 1990. This raises hopes that more information about one of the key sites in

Ruins of the *Exedra* and adjacent parts which belonged to the emperor's palace in Milan, Via Brisa / Via Gorani.

Christian history will be discovered.

The heirs of the edict

Constantine and Licinius had to come to terms with the fact that their empire was split by Diocletian in 286, a decision which was confirmed in 293. The map (page 118) shows that the division was along a line between Greece and Italy. This demarcation line ran straight through the Balkans. The consequences of this segregation led to the national and religious conflicts which has torn Yugoslavia apart, for the different parties in these conflicts are located east and west of Diocletian's ancient demarcation line.

Despite the unity displayed in

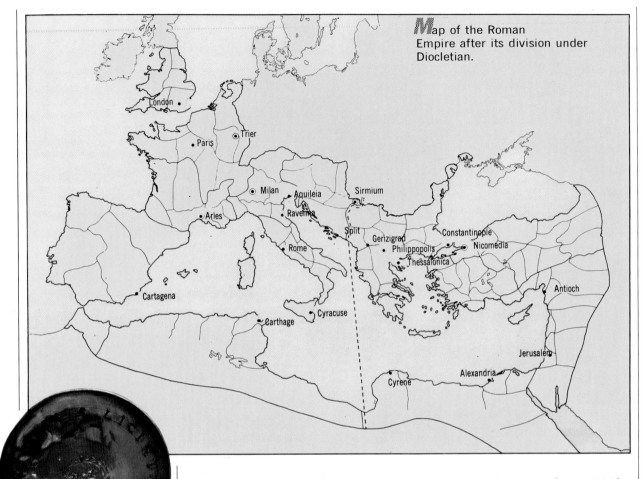

Map of the Roman Empire after its division under Diocletian.

So-called largition-plate of Licinius. This valuable gift (*largitio* = 'present', 'dedication') commemorated the tenth anniversary of Licinius taking up office in 317. The inscription at the front reads: *SIC X / SIC XX*, 'like the ten shall be the twenty (years)'. This wish is complemented by the benediction: 'O Licinius, may you always be victorious'.

Milan, war broke out between the two emperors. On 8 October 314 they fought the first battle for dominance in the Roman Empire. Constantine won the battle of Cibalae in Pannonia. In autumn 324 Licinius resigned and was exiled to Thessalonica. One year later he was executed on Constantine's order. After disposing of Licinius' son (his own nephew), Constantine ruled autocratically over the reunited Roman Empire. Only his sons Constantius and Constans stood second to him as caesars.

In front of the church of San Lorenzo Maggiore is a copy of Constantine's statue (page 119) which he erected in Rome. The original in Rome showed him holding a *labarum*, the standard with the monogram of Christ—the Chi-Rho—in a wreath in his raised right hand. Only a copy of this statue remains, with an empty right hand. It can be seen next to the old main entrance of the church of San Giovanni in Laterano in Rome, a present from Constantine to the Christians. The copy in Milan was not done very well and the right hand is empty too. Perhaps one day restorers will try to reconstruct the standard according to

Eusebius' description!

In front of the church of San Lorenzo is a colonnade which dates back to the second or third centuries AD. Sixteen columns still remain. According to contradictory sources they belonged either to a thermal spa of Maximianus, to a temple of Hercules or to a temple of Apollo. However the colonnade is interpreted, the combination of the church and this colonnade is one of the most impressive connections between Christian and non-Christian antiquity to be seen in modern Milan.

The church itself is built on foundations which were originally a Roman building. Its foundation stones were apparently taken from vacant buildings in the vicinity, particularly the amphitheatre. It is not clear yet whether the church was actually built in Constantine's time or whether it originated a few decades later, during the time of Ambrose. Its present exterior, however, dates from the late Middle Ages and later. The architecture of the central building supports an earlier date. There is evidence which suggests that the original church was built by Arians (a group which considered Christ to be only similar to God, not equal to God). Accordingly the church was taken over by the 'Orthodox' church, influenced by Rome, only after the Council of Nicaea (325). The different pictures in the *Capella di Sant'Aquilino* give no decisive evidence, for both Arians and orthodox believers could have painted Christ on a throne among the disciples, with the scrolls of the law and the Gospels at his feet (page 120). The mosaics of this particular chapel include a picture of Elijah and other prophets. Although they are not as renowned as those from Rome or Ravenna, they are

View of the modern entrance to the church of San Lorenzo Maggiore, Milan, through the columns of the second- or third-century colonnade. Between the pillars can be seen the statue of Constantine in front of the church.

Mosaic in the chapel of St Aquilinus, San Lorenzo Maggiore, first part of the fourth century; Christ, surrounded by his disciples, is enthroned above the scrolls of the law.

Close up showing the *capsa*, the container for the scrolls, at Jesus' feet.

older, and are even older than the apse mosaic of Santa Pudenziana in Rome (page 151) which is the most important from a historical point of view.

This is the first piece of art discovered so far which makes a statement about Christ's superiority over scripture: Christ is enthroned not only above the disciples, but also above the law. The later mosaic in Constantia's mausoleum in Rome (about AD 354) makes statement about church politics in depicting Christ as he entrusts Peter and Paul with the scroll of the new covenant, the New Testament. In contrast to this, the statement of the mosaic in Milan has a different emphasis. The scroll in Christ's left hand contains black mosaic stones with no text. Later, in the church of Santa Pudenziana, the equivalent picture will call him the *conservator* of the church. In contrast to the apse mosaic in Santa Pudenziana the mosaic in Milan does not highlight the significance of Peter and Paul. Only Christ rules—enthroned above the six scrolls contained in the *capsa*, the traditional container for the scrolls (picture page 120). The fact that six scrolls are depicted shows that the 'law' has now been perfected: the one Gospel (the four Gospels are seen as one unit transmitting the Good News of Jesus) has been added to the five books of Moses, the *Torah*.

A legend comes and goes

The church of Sant'Eustorgio is another of the Milan churches going back to the time of Ambrose and before. It is thought to have been founded by Bishop Eustorgio who is mentioned between 345 and 348. However, he may have been in office before that time. Its most significant development took place in the decades after Eustorgio. Nevertheless, its origin goes back to tombs from

*T*wo tombs with roofing *alla cappuccina* under the church of Sant' Eustorgio, Milan.

*S*arcophagus of the 'three wise men' (*Sepulchrum trium magorum*) in the church of Sant' Eustorgio.

the pre-Constantine period. These were found and preserved between 1959 and 1962. This entombment may have commemorated Eustorgio's predecessors. The graves were roofed with stones or tiles arranged in a triangular shape (picture above). Their simple style draws on very old practices which can be found in the

*S*hrine of the three kings in Cologne cathedral. Gold-enamel, by Nicholas of Verdun, about 1200.

necropolis of Ostia Antica and eslewhere during the first century. The two graves under Sant'Eustorgio date back to the third century. One of them contained golden earrings of a type normally manufactured to serve as tomb decoration.

The dead were buried in the ground, not cremated. This does not prove that they and their family were Christians. However, it does support this assumption, as Christians generally took over the Jewish ban on cremation practices, even if it meant that they had to use graves several times, as in this case, without removing the old bones. In other places, for example in Rome, they developed catacombs which were several miles long.

In one of the side chapels above, the big sarcophagus of the 'three wise men from the east' is displayed (picture middle page 121). According to tradition it was Helena, the emperor's mother, who dedicated them to the bishop. The inscription on it explains that this is the *Sepulchrum trium magorum*, the grave of the three magi (wise men). Yet it is only supposition that there were three of them. The number is not mentioned in the Bible; it was simply deduced from the number of presents they gave, and apart from the reference in the Gospel of Matthew there is no historical evidence for their existence. Nonetheless, various later legends try to 'fill the gaps' of our knowledge. They tell how

Helena, Constantine's mother, found the bodies and brought them to Constantinople. From there they were supposedly brought to Milan by bishop Protasius, the successor of Eustorgius.

The earliest evidence of this sarcophagus is from the ninth century. In 1162, when Friedrich Barbarossa tried to subdue Lombardy, Milan was completely destroyed, and Friedrich's chancellor, Reinald of Dassel, brought the relics of the wise men to Cologne. They arrived there on 23 July 1164 and are still displayed there in a shrine made of gold-enamel by Nicholas of Verdun (about 1200; see page 121). It was not until 1904 that some of the relics were brought back to Milan. An anthropological study showed that they date back to the first century AD, so they could be genuine, at least in theory. All the other traditions about the relics must remain speculative because the time gap between the death of these men and their discovery by Helena in the fourth century is too big. What can be deduced from this incident is the fact that Milan was not only important for the administration in the late Roman Empire, but that the early church also was eager to support the significance of this city by erecting important buildings and providing relics of New Testament characters.

The Centre is Established:
Constantine's Conquest and Archaeological Evidence of Rome's Struggle for Christian Primacy

Constantine saw himself as a Christian, and he acted accordingly, even if it meant having to demolish the family tombs of senators on Vatican Hill in order to erect the first church of St Peter above the apostle's tomb. However, he also stuck to previous convict-ions which he thought were reconcilable with his Christian faith, such as the veneration of the sun god, as a mosaic found in the catacombs on the Vatican demonstrates. This was not as surprising as it may sound. According to Scripture, Christ could in fact be seen as the one and only true sun god, and in the Constantinian era, the Roman Church looked for forms of expression in art and archi-tecture which would appeal to the non-Christian 'intelligentsia'.

Christ as Helios (sun god). Fourth-century mosaic in the Vatican Catacombs.

*B*ust of Constantine the Great, *Palazzo dei Conservatori* in Rome.

A clash with the senate

Rome had declined in significance after Diocletian's administrative reforms, when the empire was ruled from other cities. Nevertheless, the senate and the people of Rome were still highly respected. Only after he had conquered Rome could Constantine claim dominion over the entire western empire and ultimately the whole Roman Empire. His victory over Licinius in the battle of Chrysopolis on 18 September 324 was the most important success strategically. However, the decisive psychological effect for the population in the Roman Empire was achieved through his victory over Maxentius at the Milvian Bridge north-west of Rome (see picture). Maxentius drowned in the River Tiber, and on 28 October 312 Constantine led his troops into Rome, with the Chi-Rho on their standards.

He immediately offended the Roman senate by refusing to perform the traditional sacrifice to Jupiter on the Capitol, an act expected of every victor. This was a deliberate sign. The tenth anniversary of his office as Augustus was celebrated for several days in July 315. Again, neither on this occasion nor at the next anniversary ten years later did he sacrifice to Jupiter. Even two hundred years later Zosimus, a non-Christian historian, pointed out that this negligence by Constantine demonstrated an unwholesome departure from the old traditions and that the embracing of Christianity led to Rome's decline. Nonetheless, Constantine was not primarily concerned with denying old traditions. He did away only with those rites which were in direct opposition to his Christian faith as, for example, sacrifices to other deities. He did not resist

*T*he Milvian Bridge (*Pons Milvius*). It was converted into a stone bridge in AD109. Here Constantine won the battle against Maxentius on 28 October 312. The four central arches are still preserved.

vanity, for he erected oversized monuments of himself—this was part of the rules for a monarch. Yet he clearly refused any deification of his own person. A typical example is the bust in the *Palazzo dei Conservatori* in Rome (page 124).

The triumphal arch (picture above) which the senate dedicated to Constantine in 315 displays no Christian symbolism at all. It has now been restored, and further information may be gained from continuing excavations in the vicinity. It is clear that the senate tried to demonstrate their traditional beliefs here, for Constantine is depicted as sacrificing to the gods. Was this a subtle revenge for Constantine's refusal to sacrifice to Jupiter? Constantine hit back by erecting the statue which showed him with the *labarum*, the standard with the monogram of Christ, in his raised right hand (pages 110–11).

The politics behind the pictures

We have already encountered the phenomenon of sun worship in connection with the cult of Mithras and at the northern wall of the church of St Gereon in Cologne. These were ambiguous examples which could be interpreted in different ways. The mosaic discovered in Münster-Sarnsheim near the River Nahe in Germany appears to be unequivocal. This mid third-

century work depicts Helios/Sol with his fiery chariot surrounded by the twelve signs of the Zodiac (picture above).

At first sight, this seems to point to a purely pagan context. However, a third-century Christian acquainted with the Jewish tradition of the Old Testament would have reacted differently. For a long time such a 'sun chariot' with its horses stood in the Temple in Jerusalem, a present of the kings of Judah. It was finally destroyed by King Josiah. Yet these objects were mentioned again and again in Jewish writings later than the Old Testament. Archaeological discoveries in Hammat-iberias and the synagogue of Beth-Alpha show that Jewish art used this pictorial language, including signs of the Zodiac, during New Testament times and after. The

Constantine's arch from the west. With a height of 21m, a depth of 7.40 m and a width of 5.70m it is the largest independent monument of imperial Rome.

God used parts of contemporary culture for his purposes, as for example in the incident when he enabled the magi (astronomers) of a Babylonian observatory to calculate the orbit of the Star of Bethlehem and find the birthplace of the Messiah. For the people of the time stars were important signals, as can be seen from the reaction of Herod. However, this in no way indicates that stars were worshipped.

Constantine, and Christian artists contemporary with him, knew this. There are no illustrations showing the sun god with the signs of the Zodiac as part of the Christian religion. Christian art displayed the radical change in interpretation of symbols: only Christ is the true

*F*loor mosaic of the sun-god Sol/Helios in Münster—Sarmsheim, middle of the third century AD.

*C*hrist as sun god. Mosaic on the ceiling of a mausoleum in the Vatican necropolis. It was first discovered and described by Tiberio Alfarano in 1574.

picture from Beth-Alpha is particularly interesting. Apart from its Hebrew inscription it is so similar to the mosaic from Münster-Sarnsheim that they are interchangeable. In its centre is the sun god with his chariot, surrounded by a sky with stars which symbolizes day and night. In the corners are the four seasons.

A subtle distinction had to be observed. Although according to the book of Genesis Jews could read 'signs' in the sky, according to the book of Deuteronomy they were not allowed to worship them! Jewish history shows that this distinction was not always observed. A similar distinction was also necessary for Christians.

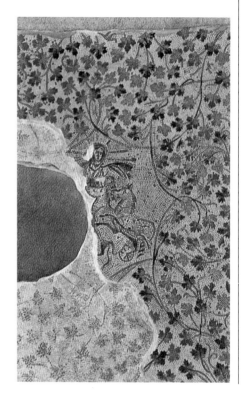

sun, as can be seen in St Gereon or the necropolis on Vatican Hill.

Since Aurelius (270–75) the nimbus, or arc of the sun round the head, had been part of the portraiture of Roman rulers, corresponding to the nimbus of *Sol invictus*, the invincible sun god. Nonetheless, from 324— even before the Council of Nicaea—Constantine abolished this symbol on all coins and other representations of his person. He also dropped the epithet *invictus*, for it was too closely related to the cult of the sun god. One connection between Christ and the sun still visible today is the fact that his resurrection is not celebrated on the Sabbath, but on Sun-day, the *Dies Solis*.

The oldest known representation of Mary with Jesus

gives another indication of how Christianity incorporated the heavenly bodies in its belief (page 127). In the catacomb of Priscilla there is a fresco which depicts the prophet Balaam before the sitting Virgin Mary. He prophesies the coming of the Messiah: 'A star will come out of Jacob; a sceptre will rise out of Israel.' This fresco originated at the same time as the mosaic with the sun god from Münster-Sarmsheim.

Rome becomes a city of churches

Even before the edict of Milan, Constantine planned a systematic church building project in Rome. The first step was the construction of a church within the city walls. As its location he chose a house which was already in his possession, the *Domus Faustae*. The adjacent barracks of a cavalry guard was also knocked down, and the church erected was called the Lateran Basilica. To this day it has the status of 'mother and head of all churches of the city and the globe'. Thus, formally it is even more important than the church of St Peter on the Vatican (see above). It has been destroyed several times and so changed significantly in the course of time, and its modern shape was formed in the seventeenth century. However, the interior still gives a clue to its original outline.

LEFT: Altar for the 'invincible Sun God'. Above the head with the typical nimbus is the dedication INVICTO/SOLI.

ABOVE: Fresco with the prophet Balaam before Mary with Jesus. Catacomb of Priscilla; mid-third century AD, perhaps older.

Constantine intended the outline of the imperial basilica with the typical reception hall used in this church to portray Christ as the true ruler. With its length of 98m and a width of 56m this 'reception hall' demonstrated Christ's sovereignty impressively.

Next door he erected a baptistry (see picture) above an original pagan site (see pages 96–98). It had a circular outline surrounded by pillars. The

*T*he modern Lateran Basilica with the baptistry to the right.

*M*ap of the seven church districts in Rome including some of the important ancient church buildings. These are re-presented by crosses: 1 = Church of St Peter; 2 = Santi Cosmas e Damiano; 4= Santa Pudenziana 5 = Santa Maria Maggiore; 6 = San Giovanni in Later-ano (Lateran Basilica); 7 = Santo Stefano Rotondo; 8 = Santi Giovanni e Paolo; 9 = Santa Sabina; 10 = San Paolo fuori le Mura; 14 = San Sebas-tiano ad Catacumbas; 18 = San Lorenzo fuori le Mura; 19 = Sant' Agnese fuori le Mura. The trian-gles represent catacombs.

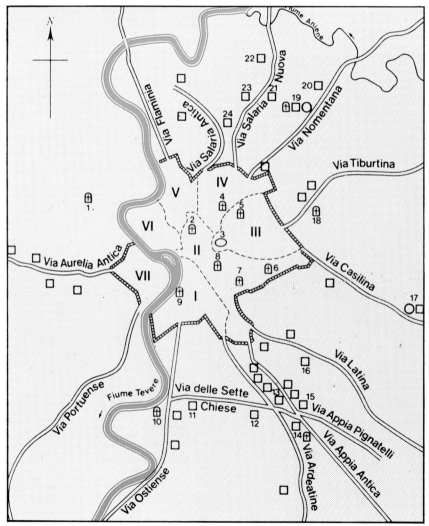

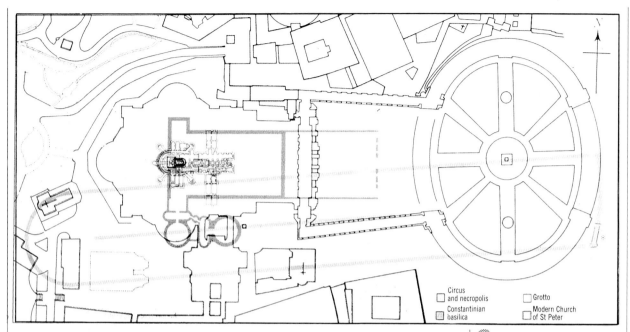

Circus and necropolis — Constantinian basilica — Grotto — Modern Church of St Peter

piscina (baptismal pool) was reached by stairs. This circular style influenced Christian architecture for a long time. Its present outline, however, is due to Pope Sixtus III who converted the circular building into an octagon in 435. He also made some changes inside, but the red porphyry pillars and the basic outline of the *piscina* as well as other details of the original Constantinian building survived.

Santa Croce in Gerusalemme is another large church which Constantine erected inside the city walls (see page 135). It also was built on the site belonging to the emperor. The original house on it had been erected by the emperor Elagabalus (218–22). Later it was the residence of Constantine's mother Helena, until she and Constantine converted it into this church. In doing so, they used the large hall

(39m by 25m floor space and 22m high) whose northern wall can still be seen outside.

The Church of St Peter

However, the most successful building was Constantine's first church of St Peter on Vatican Hill

Sketch of the church of St Peter in its ancient and present shape with Nero's circus and the cemetery on Vatican Hill.

Isometric outline of Peter's grave (below the Trophy of Gaius) and its vicinity.

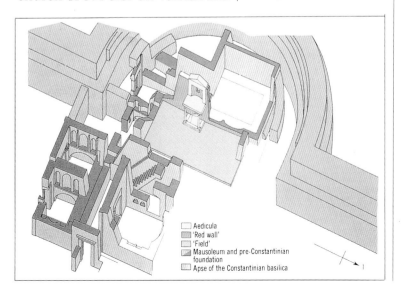

Aedicula — 'Red wall' — 'Field' — Mausoleum and pre-Constantinian foundation — Apse of the Constantinian basilica

*F*resco of the longitudinal section of Constantine's church of St Peter by Domenico Tasseli, late sixteenth century.

(sketches above and below; draft page 130; photograph page 131). The sketch which outlines the building's history (see above) shows its location and the architectural problems connected with it. It was adjacent to Nero's circus and in the middle of a large cemetery, the authentic site of Peter's grave. Therefore the church could be built above it only if parts of the hill were flattened and other graves were opened, filled in or destroyed. These architectural problems may have contributed to the time it took to finish the building (from 321 to 349). The determined efforts to complete the building despite these difficulties is another argument for the care taken to use an authentic site (see chapter 1).

The sketch at the bottom of the page shows how difficult it was to build the church above the Trophy of Gaius, the monument above Peter's grave mentioned by the historian Eusebius. Details of the excavation report are still disputed among archaeologists, but this sketch is accepted as a reliable reconstruction of Constantine's original building activity.

A fresco by Domenico Tasseli from the late sixteenth century shows what Constantine's finished building looked like before new building activities started under Pope Julius II in 1506 which gave the church its present form (picture page 130). The separation wall at the end of the three naves which is visible on the picture was installed in 1538 in order to allow worship in the church while construction work was still continuing. Only a few remains from Constantine's era are still preserved in the grottoes and cemetery of Vatican Hill. The amazing size of the new building almost hides the fact that the original church was Constantine's largest building in Rome with a length of 91m, a width of 63.5m and a height of 38.5m.

Churches over meeting places

Occasionally it has been said that Constantine's plan to give Rome's architecture a Christian style actually failed, for his three largest buildings were located on the outskirts of Rome on his own land. However, this criticism

View of Michelangelo's Dome with the Latin text of Matthew 16:18–19 including the key phrase *Tu es Petrus* – 'You are Peter'.

misses the point. By converting or even demolishing buildings in his own possession the emperor clearly demonstrated that his whole household had become Christian. This was an important example and encouragement for Christians in Rome. It led to Christian communities all over Rome beginning to build churches above their old meeting places (see map on page 128). Constantine's building activities were also a challenge to the Roman élite and the senate.

The statue of Peter (page 132) in front of the Vatican grottoes must have had a similar effect. The apostle is portrayed like a philosopher (or a senator). In fact, the original statue had indeed depicted a philosopher or senator. It was changed into Peter's statue by adding a new left hand with a key and a new head. The halo was added later. Once more we see a deliberate substitution of Christianity for the old traditions which were 'obsolete and ageing'.

Pre-Christian seated figure of a philosopher or senator, changed in Constantine's time into the apostle Peter by the addition of a new left hand and a new head.

The Holy Land Beckons:
The Emperor's Mother Helena and her Discoveries

It was Helena, Constantine's mother, who practically invented archaeology. On her trip to the Holy Land, in 323, she looked for and was given 'true relics', such as the cross of Christ and the 'Holy Stairs' which Jesus walked up on his way to Pilate in the praetorium. While the cross was lost in the Crusades, the stairs are still in Rome, and even Martin Luther climbed up them on his knees, as do many pious pilgrims to this very day. But how reliable are these finds of Christian archaeology? Where does legend end and history begin?

The *Scala Santa* or 'Holy Stairs' in Rome. There are ordinary stairs to the left and right; the central staircase may only be ascended on one's knees.

A greatly respected lady

When Helena died at the end of 329 she was about eighty years old, and she was buried in Rome with all honours. Formerly a *stabularia*, owner of a guest house, from a modest background, she had been raised to the status of Augusta (empress) by her son in 325. She was laid to rest in her own mausoleum near the catacomb of Santi Marcellino e Pietro at the Via Labicana (picture below) in a costly porphyry sarcophagus, today kept in a Vatican museum (page 135). Although her grave was located outside the city wall, it was not in an insignificant place. The cemetery of the catacomb of SS Marcellino e Pietro was the most splendid of its kind in Rome. It was

*H*elena's mausoleum near the catacomb of Santi Marcellino e Pietro, Via Labicana, Rome.

discovered at the beginning of this century and today is accessible only for scholarly research. The pictures painted on the walls are arranged to explain Christian values. Many scenes from the New Testament are depicted, some arranged like a cycle of stories. Frescoes which highlighted Christian superiority over pre-Christian symbolism were also central to Constantine's politics displayed in art, and surely the same was true for his mother. Examples are a 'Good Shepherd', a 'praying' Orpheus and—of course—Christ as sun god.

Helena's mausoleum was adjacent to the cemetery basilica and covered parts of the catacombs. The few remains still visible to the superficial observer give little idea of the large size of the buildings. Originally Constantine wanted to be buried here as well. The main excavations were conducted by Friedrich Deichmann (1940 and 1954–58) and the Ecole Française (begun in 1975, still continuing in some areas). They have revealed that the architecture was similar to the basilicas on the cemeteries of San Sebastiano ad Catacumba (Via Appia) and Sant'Agnese fuori le Mura (Via Nomentana).

The size of the buildings was far from modest. The basilica had a length of 65m, a width of 23m and a height of 14m. It was an extraordinarily large building for its purpose, especially as it could not be used as a church, for its whole floor was taken up by graves. Furthermore, there was a large atrium just east of the basilica. This building was 28.5m by 9.5m square and was the same height as the basilica. Helena's mausoleum was adjacent to the atrium. It is the only ruin still visible above floor level today (page 134). The circular building was 25.5m high. Its inner diameter was 20.18m and its outer diameter 27.74 m. However, these mere figures cannot reveal the original splendour of this architectural masterpiece with its rich interior. They only hint at the impressive monument where Helena was buried, just three years after her triumphant return from the Holy Land.

A home for the hoard

The story of Helena's discovery of the three crosses (of Jesus and the two criminals crucified with him) in Jerusalem was handed down to us by Ambrose, bishop of Milan. He mentions it in his book *De Obitu Theodosii*, 'On the Death of Theodosius', which he wrote in 395. Helena recognized the true cross of Christ because of the *titulus*, the trilingual inscription on it mentioned in the Gospel of John. As we see in chapter 2, Ambrose was closely connected with the emperor's court and was thus well informed.

The gist of this record is supported by Rufinus, theologian and translator of Origen's works, who lived in Jerusalem from 378 to 397. He tells how Helena had difficulty in identifying the place where Christ was crucified because it lay buried beneath a temple to Venus. This comment has been substantiated by archaeology. After a 50cm thick layer of lime mortar had been removed, the ruins of the upper part of this temple were found in 1991. These ruins were immediately next to a hole in the ground where the middle cross must have stood. Apparently the emperor Hadrian levelled out the hill of Golgotha some time after AD135 in order to build the Venus sanctuary here, when he had crushed the revolt of the Jewish

Helena's porphyry sarcophagus from her mausoleum; today kept in the Pio Clement Museum of the Vatican. It is decorated not with Christian or pagan motifs, but with victorious Roman soldiers and defeated 'barbarians'.

Reliquary with a wooden
piece supposed to be from
the Cross of Christ. In
1858 the French author
Ernest Hello calculated
that even twice the
amount of all relics of the
cross known worldwide
would only add up to a
tenth of a typical ancient
cross.

leader Bar-Kochba.

The upper part which has
been laid open is in fact quite
narrow. The area where the two
crosses to the left and right must
have been was eroded. This
archaeological discovery means
that Rufinus' and Ambrose's
remarks need to be re-evaluated,
for until then there had been
almost unanimous scholarly
consensus that the story about
Helena's discovery of the cross
was a legend which originated
after her death. Seemingly
important evidence for this
opinion was the fact that, among
other authors, Eusebius,
Constantine's court historian,
did not mention Helena's
discovery.

However, there is a
convincing explanation for
Eusebius' omission. He was
bishop in Caesarea, which traced

its origins back to the apostle
Philip. Until 326, Caesarea, with
the biggest Christian library in
the empire, had been much more
influential than Jerusalem. As
Caesarea could not provide
authentic relics, Eusebius was
afraid that his residence might
lose its influence to Jerusalem.
This fear was evidently justified;
Constantine started extensive
building activities in Jerusalem
only a few years later. Therefore
it can be assumed that Eusebius'
Church History does not
disprove Helena's discovery; he
does not deny it, but he omits it
for his own reasons. In another
case he followed a similar
procedure, this time not for his
own purposes, but in order to
spare the emperor some
embarrassment: the execution of
Crispus and Fausta. If he was our
only source of information, we

would know nothing about these deaths.

In the light of these discoveries it is necessary to reconsider the scholarly verdict mentioned above. Even Rufinus' remark that Helena sent some of the relics to her son can be taken more seriously as a result. Could it be that some of the relics which are presently kept in the church of Santa Croce in Gerusalemme (pictures page 136) do actually go back to Helena? Is it possible that they are authentic?

The name of the church, 'Holy Cross in Jerusalem', is an affirmative statement in itself. Helena's finds are kept in a side chapel there. (The modern interior of this chapel is shaped by the influence of Mussolini's Italian Fascism.) The individual relics are the vertical bar from the cross of the repentant criminal, a part of Christ's cross (picture

Reliquary believed to contain two thorns of Christ's crown of thorns.

page 136), two thorns from the crown of thorns (picture above), a nail from the cross (picture on right), part of the apostle Thomas' forefinger (supposedly

Reliquary believed to contain a nail from the Cross of Christ.

Reliquary believed to contain part of Thomas' forefinger.

the one with which he touched Jesus' side; picture page 137), the *titulus* (see above) from the cross, as well as some other objects. Naturally, the modern visitor will consider some of these objects to be mere curiosities, not to mention the forefinger! However, it is exactly this rather unlikely relic which is not mentioned in the early reports on Helena's finds. Obviously it was added later, an expression of more excessive belief in relics.

Another interesting question is: how could the three crosses be found in the first place if they were buried under a temple? It is hard to imagine that they were still there when Hadrian built his temple above them one hundred years after the crucifixion. This is especially doubtful considering the fact that there was a severe shortage of wood in this area of the Roman Empire. (In AD70 the Romans were desperate for wood to be used for siege machines in order to conquer Jerusalem.) However, it is exactly this shortage which might explain their survival. Golgotha was frequently used for crucifixions. Reports from other parts of the empire also testify to the fact that the vertical bars of crosses were used again and again; only the horizontal bars were changed. Thus the 'cross' which Christ carried was 'only' the horizontal bar—which, of course, was still unbearably heavy for a tortured man.

The timespan between the

crucifixion and Hadrian's temple is so great that it is in fact unlikely that the crosses there survived. Yet it is not impossible that they did stand there until Hadrian took them down in order to build his temple to Venus. Rufinus recounted how Helena demolished the temple and found the crosses 'in disorder' and 'buried deep below the rubble'. This part of Rufinus' account seems reliable, notably because his description of the site has been substantiated by recent archaeology (see above). Yet there is another touch in Rufinus' report which casts doubt on its reliability. He stressed God's 'miraculous' intervention in the discovery and identification of the cross of Christ. After Helena had interrogated citizens from Jerusalem about the location of Golgotha the exact spot was revealed to her by a 'sign from heaven' associated with the heavenly sign of the monogram of Christ which her son saw before he affixed it to his soldiers' shields. The following remark, however, is even stranger. According to Rufinus, Helena was not even content with the identification of the cross when the *titulus* was found. Rufinus stated that in such a doubtful case the uncertainty demanded clarification by divine evidence. Macarios, bishop of Jerusalem, advised Helena to bring the three crosses to a sick lady. Touching the authentic cross of Christ would bring her healing. The first two crosses produced no effect, but the third cross brought instant healing.

It is important for us today to enter into the frame of thought of the ancient world. For a modern historian archaeological facts would be sufficient. Yet for the people of the New Testament (compare the miracles which happened when people touched Jesus or Paul) and Constantine's era, miracles were just as important as archaeological facts. Does that invalidate their accounts?

The ring from the cross

At the end of 1991 Greek archaeologists Georg Lavas and Saki Mitropoulos made another important discovery in this area. While excavating the original rock of Golgotha they found a hollow behind the present altar there. In it was a stone ring which may have held the cross in its position (picture above). Is it the ring from the Cross of Christ, or was it placed there by Helena as a souvenir? Investigations of the ring and its dating have not yet been completed.

It was not mentioned in any of the early sources. On the one hand, this may be due to the fact that the ring was not venerated because it was not part of the cross proper. On the other hand, it can be assumed that the ring would have been adored and provided with another legend had it been 'invented' at the time

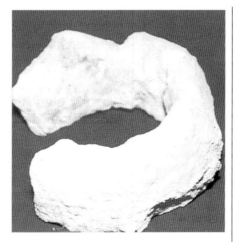

The cross ring in the hollow behind the altar on Golgotha (top picture) and after it was laid open (bottom).

of Helena or on another occasion. The fact that the ring has a diameter of only 11.5cm is another reason which makes invention unlikely, for if this ring was used in connection with the cross it could not have been higher than 2.5m. Yet a later

The Church of the Holy Sepulchre today. The steps outside lead up to the authentic rock of Golgotha which until 1991 had been covered by a layer of lime mortar.

as nothing like it was mentioned in crucifixion accounts. Apart from that, the ring makes the curious story about Bishop Macarios more plausible as well. A cross with a length of 2.5m fits into a room of an ill person much more easily than the monumental crosses portrayed for us throughout the history of art.

In conclusion it may be said that in the earliest and best historical sources, the weirdest relics—the 'Holy Stair', the horizontal bar from the criminal's cross, the thorns and Thomas' forefinger—are not connected with Helena. (In recent years the real location of Pilate's praetorium from which the presumed 'Holy Stair' stemmed was discovered as part of the lower palace of the Hasmoneans.) This excessive belief in relics cannot be attributed to Helena. However, the authenticity of the discoveries which were ascribed to her, like the cross with the *titulus* and some nails, has been supported by recent archaeological research. (The nails may have been kept somewhere else, for Joseph of Arimathea took Jesus from the cross.) There is no objective proof, yet the results of future investigations may lead to greater certainty. The evidence mentioned above, nonetheless, substantiates the story of Helena's relics in such a way that they can no longer be considered mere legend. They are historically conceivable.

inventor would not have missed the chance to highlight that Jesus was 'lifted up', as explained in John's Gospel, on a high cross, so he would have chosen a bigger ring, to testify to a bigger cross corresponding to the size imagined throughout the history of art. The invention of such a floor fastening, especially a circular one, is also implausible

Imperial Christianity and its Remains:

Constantine Establishes and Protects the Sites

Constantine initiated a building programme in Jerusalem which was intended to protect the sites marking the events of Jesus' last days on earth—most notably Golgotha, the empty tomb and the place of the ascension. While the ascension could of course not be confirmed archaeologically, the sites of Golgotha and the empty tomb have remained objects of scientific investigation. The graffito of a pilgrim's ship found in the Chapel of St Vartan beneath the Church of the Holy Sepulchre points to the veneration of the site from the earliest days of Christian pilgrimage.

Domine ivimus, 'Lord, we have arrived.' A pilgrim's graffito of a ship beneath the Church of the Holy Sepulchre. Its dating is still highly controversial; some date it to the Constantinian period, others before AD135, when Jerusalem was destroyed by Hadrian.

The Chapel of St Vartan with the pilgrim's graffito, protected behind a glass cover.

A discovery with important consequences

The Armenian excavators under the supervision of their bishop Guregh Kapikian did not expect sensational discoveries, when they continued excavation work once they had finished a joint project with Israeli archaeologists in their part of the Church of the Holy Sepulchre. Nevertheless, they suddenly found a hollow space behind a wall. It is now laid open and restored and has been given the name 'St Vartan and the Armenian Martyrs'. It represents a very unusual discovery which is still not completely understood.

On one of the walls was a drawing of a ship with a tilted (or broken) mast. Below was the Latin inscription 'DOMINE IVIMUS', written in clumsy letters (see pages 141–42). The ship's significance, the correct meaning of the inscription and its date are still matters of controversy. What is clear, however, is that it has a Christian background; it calls on the Lord after a successful sea journey. Apparently the pilgrim arrived in the vicinity of Golgotha and the empty tomb, but not at the sites themselves. If drawing and text originated at about the time when Constantine built the church, they would be the first evidence of pilgrimages to the Holy Land known to us. Nonetheless, this would not be very exciting, as pilgrimages to the historical sites of Jesus' life were promoted by Constantine and his mother, and were thus quite a common feature of the time.

However, even this already late dating is still disputed by some critics who accuse the discoverers of having forged or manipulated the find in order to arrive at a Christian interpretation. Before its restoration, in 1975, a member of the British School of Archaeology identified the letters of the inscription as ISIS MYRIONIMOS. Yet this reading before the restoration seems to be a product of fantasy. An English translation would be: 'Isis of the thousandfold names', consequently this text would not have any link whatsoever to the picture in question. In addition, it would also be wrong grammatically, for, as numerous other examples show, the correct spelling would be the form ISIDI. When Immanuele Testa, an Italian Catholic, restored and cleaned the inscription he read DOMINE IVIMUS.

The earlier interpreters were indignant and charged Testa with fraud. An investigation by the Criminal Investigation Bureau, a branch of Israel's national police, finally established the integrity of his work on 12 January 1977. Interestingly, this has not been the only occasion when the Israelis settled a controversy between Gentile scholars. On another occasion they analyzed the papyrus fragment 7Q5 found in Qumran cave 7 and made visible the trace of a crucial letter, and on 12 April 1992 they finally established that this small fragment was part of the Gospel of Mark. This is another hypothesis which had long been disputed by scholars, for if this fragment really belongs to Mark's Gospel it would have far-ranging consequences. Firstly, the origin

of the Gospel must be dated before AD68. Secondly, it would mean that the early Christian church spread the gospel among the Essenes from Qumran.

Even if the pilgrim ship under the Church of the Holy Sepulchre originated from the time before Constantine it would not have the same consequences as the interpretation of the Qumran

*T*he drawing of the ship with the inscription **DOMINE IVIMUS**. The ship has been identified as a Roman merchant ship. The sail is rolled up behind the mast, bound together with red ropes. The ship's bow has the shape of a goose's head.

*E*mperor Hadrian (AD117–38). Copy of a bust from Hadrian's mausoleum in Rome. Munich, Glyptothek.

143

The fault caused by an earthquake (cf. Matthew 27:51f.). It was recovered in 1991.

The present Church of the Holy Sepulchre. Presumably, remains of Hadrian's temple to Venus have been incorporated in its upper arches and decoration.

fragment. Nevertheless, according to recent findings it is still very interesting evidence for Christian activities in Jerusalem.

Hadrian changed the city in a significant way. The fact that the pilgrim could not reach Golgotha or the empty tomb directly hints at the ship's date of origin. It must be later than AD135, for in that year Hadrian built temples on both sites so that Christians could not visit the holy places any more. On the other hand, it is earlier than 326, the year when Constantine (and his mother Helena) demolished those temples so that all believers could visit the sites freely again.

The wall on which the drawing is sketched dates back to the first century, so that its dating does not help in the interpretation of the drawing. The ship's construction could belong to the second, the third or even the early fourth century. However, the inscription may give further clues. It is written in Latin. This is quite unusual, for Greek was the common language spoken in the eastern empire well into the Middle Ages. Thus it may be assumed that its writer came from the west, possibly from Rome. Again, the normal written language in Rome until the latter half of the second century was Greek. Latin became common among literate Christians like Minucius Felix, Tertullian or the author of the *Scillitan Martyrdom* after about AD165–180, though it is possible that isolated inscriptions in Latin were written earlier. The SATOR AREPO / PATERNOSTER inscription from Pompeii (see page 93–94) from AD79, which some scholars now accept as Christian, would be a very early example.

The text's content is another clue. Translated literally, DOMINE IVIMUS means: 'Lord, we have arrived.' There is a clear connection with the drawing, since the tilted or possibly broken mast signifies that the ship had arrived at its journey's destination.

Yet again, some scholars look for more sophisticated explanations. Magen Broshi from Israel and Dominican Pierre Benoit suggest reading *ibimus* because in late Latin 'v' and 'b' were pronounced in the same way. The text's translation would then be 'we will go', an allusion

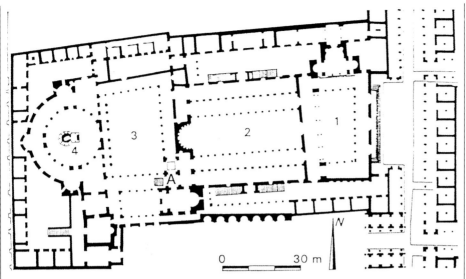

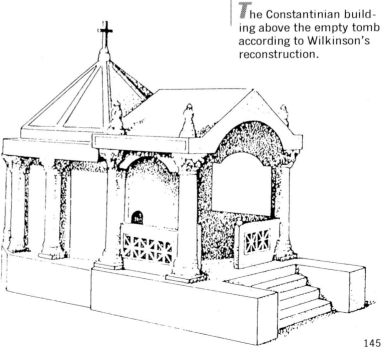

Sketch of Constantine's Church of the Holy Sepulchre reconstructed by Couäsnon in 1968. 4 = the area of the Empty Tomb; 3 = inner atrium; 2 = Martyrion and Chapel of Helena (to the east are the steps which lead down to the Chapel of St Vartan); 1 = outer atrium; A = Golgotha.

to the Latin text of Psalm 122:1: *In domum Domine ibimus*, 'Let us [or: we shall] go to the house of the Lord'. However, this emendation is not really an improvement, for according to the picture the pilgrim(s) have already arrived and an allusion to Psalm 122 is possible with the perfect form *ivimus* of the original anyway. The German scholar Gerhard-Wilhelm Nebe has suggested the text is an allusion to Jesus' calming of the storm, notably a rather free quotation from the Latin versions of Luke 8:24 and Matthew 8:25: *Lord, we are perishing.' Nebe would read ire* as meaning *perire* and 'v' instead of 'b': *perivimus*, 'we are perishing'. However, this very elaborate hypothesis then has to explain why the author of the text only occasionally made use of correct Latin grammar.

It seems reasonable to ask, however, why should the simplest solution not be the right one: text and drawing mean what they plainly communicate? Another possibility would be to understand the ship allegorically. Is the ship in a figurative sense a picture of the persecuted Christian church, a symbol known to the early church fathers?

The Constantinian building above the empty tomb according to Wilkinson's reconstruction.

*P*resent-day *aedicula* above the empty tomb, with scaffolding from 1934.

*I*nterior of the present-day Chapel of the Empty Tomb

An apparently simple discovery—a clearly visible drawing and an accurately restored and fully preserved inscription—has suddenly

View across from the German Lutheran Church of the Redeemer to the Church of the Holy Sepulchre.

become the centre of controversy. This case shows that complicated reconstructions are neither helpful nor necessary and at times wrong conclusions can be drawn from mistaken premises. It seems more appropriate to treat the archaeological evidence seriously and combine it with the most satisfactory linguistic interpretation. This leads to a dating before the time of Constantine. (During or after his time the drawing would not have had any significance in this locality, as the sites would have been easy to visit.) On the other hand, its date must be after the erection of Hadrian's temple. The most convincing solution seems to be a date towards the end of the second or at the beginning of the third century. During this time Christians were not intentionally persecuted in the two empires. In the west Latin was commonly spoken and written. About AD180 colourful descriptions of early Christianity came into fashion and pilgrims may have been prompted by them to visit the Holy Land for themselves.

Despite all the controversies it is clear that the discovery of the drawing and text in the Chapel of St Vartan gives further clues to archaeological and historical considerations in connection with Golgotha and the empty tomb, as well as the history of the buildings on site. If nothing else it is further evidence that a firm local tradition about these important Christian sites existed even at a time when it was impossible to visit them directly. It was this tradition which directed Helena and Constantine.

A signal to the world

Constantine had built three main churches in Rome: the Lateran Basilica, the Church of St Peter and the Church of the Holy Cross (Santa Croce in Gerusalemme). He also built three main churches in the Holy Land: the Church of Jesus' Nativity, the church above the Empty Tomb (and Golgotha) and the church

function on several occasions. In modern times it is considered to be the place where Jesus taught the Lord's Prayer.

It was not until 1910 that remains of Constantine's building were found there. Investigations in Bethlehem and at the Church of the Holy Sepulchre reveal that, like the Church of St Peter in Rome, Constantine carefully

View across the twelfth-century church of St Mary Latin (formerly the church of a German order of crusaders) on the Temple Mount to the Mount of Olives.

on the Mount of Olives, the so-called *Eleona*. The latter building was probably just an afterthought, possibly to arrive at the number three which symbolizes the Trinity. The exact location where Jesus made his speech about the end of the age and the place of his ascension on the Mount of Olives had never been identified, and the church there changed its memorial

investigated the sites before he began construction work. When he was sure of the locations' authenticity he started to build in grand style. As in Rome, where he demolished parts of an old cemetery in order to build the church of St Peter, he now did not hesitate to demolish Hadrian's temple. He even sent a letter to Macarios, the bishop of Jerusalem, stating that this church should commemorate Christ's resurrection and that it should surpass all other churches in glory and splendour. He ordered Macarios to send him a list of craftsmen, building materials and costs, promising that he would provide everything.

Constantine was aware of the fact that, as when he built the church of St Peter in Rome, such pro-Christian policies would not go unchallenged. The majority in the Roman Empire did not yet subscribe to the Christian faith. Notably state officials and aristocracy still clung to the old cults. At about the same time, about 325, the emperor sent a decree to the governors and high officials who were still apparently pagan. In it he explicitly prohibited them to make sacrifices or to commit idolatry (*eidololatria*)in any other way. It is important to keep this resistance to his projects in mind in order to appreciate how important it was for Constantine to examine the historicity of these sites very thoroughly. He could not risk his opponents later accusing him of following mere legends and myths.

Modern archaeology is increasingly successful in supporting Constantine's identification of the historical sites of Christianity. In Bethlehem it can be demonstrated that the cave where Christ's birthplace is venerated was in fact part of a dwelling cave of the early period

of the New Testament. Similarly, more and more evidence concerning the Church of the Holy Sepulchre is being gathered. Here we not only have the hollow where the cross ring was found (see previous chapter). There is also the crack which goes right through the rock of Golgotha (see page 139) down to the so-called 'Chapel of Adam'. According to competent archaeologists this crack supports the report about an earthquake in the Gospel of Matthew. This earthquake followed the crucifixion and made the 'rocks split'. Major parts of the history of the Church of the Holy Sepulchre can now be reconstructed (sketch page 145). It can also be proved that Golgotha and the empty tomb, as well as another tomb nearby which can be visited in the Syrian Chapel, were outside the city wall of Jesus' time. This also corresponds to the accounts in the Gospels. Another investigation using most advanced methods in order to trace the history of the empty tomb from Jesus' burial until today is still continuing. Results from this investigation will be especially interesting.

Professor Michael Cooper and Professor Martin Biddle, two British scholars, are gathering thousands of photographs of each detail of all the stones still preserved in the empty tomb. They are entered into a photometric programme which will recreate every building period of the site on a computer screen. These computer-aided reconstructions will show whether earlier reconstructions, like the sketch of the empty tomb in the fourth century by Wilkinson (see picture page 145), are correct or not. The outside of the empty tomb, barely kept together by scaffolding provided in 1934 during the period of British mandate (page 146) reveals how necessary a comprehensive restoration of the building is. A project to take apart the whole building stone by stone in order to rebuild it has been authorized. Before this is done, Biddle and Cooper hope to record all possible details and analyze them. Their project is sure to produce reliable data about the site's original appearance (page 146).

The background

A view across to the Mount of Olives with the *Eleona* reveals how much of the evidence for early Christianity still awaits investigation. In the foreground is a threefold structure from the twelfth century with a hospice, church and hospital erected by German crusaders. During Jesus' time this was the site of the north-west corner of the lower palace of the Hasmoneans, the old Jewish royal family. This is where Pilate's praetorium, the place where Jesus was sentenced to be crucified, really was. In the centre is the Temple Mount with the El Aksa Mosque. To the right was the double gate through which Jesus, like every other pious Jew, entered the temple, by the ancient stairs which have been revealed just recently. His worship, his speech about the end of the age, his lament about Jerusalem, his death sentence and his resurrection come to mind. Yet some traces of his life can be illuminated only by archaeology, imperial buildings and modern reconstructions.

Jerusalem or Rome?
Remnants of Unity in Diversity

*During the fourth century, Christianity had permeated
all levels of society all over the empire, but it had lost
contact with its Jewish Christian origins in the process. At
the same time, people in Rome were trying to preserve
an accurate memory of its beginnings in Jerusalem.
Investigations have shown that the apse mosaic at Santa
Pudenziana faithfully portrays the historical sites as they
were known in the fourth century.*

Santa Pudenziana, Rome. Apse mosaic with Christ and the apostles, and two
women representing the 'Church of the Circumcision' and the 'Church of the
Gentiles', in front of the Cross on Golgotha, the original Church of the Holy
Sepulchre (*Anastasis*, left) and the Church of the Ascension (right).

Back to the roots

In August 410 Rome was conquered, for the first time in almost 1000 years. Alaric, king of the Western Goths, looted the city for three days. Alaric was a Christian himself, but he was an Arian and therefore also a religious opponent of Rome. However, he spared all religious buildings. It was an exception to his policy when some of his soldiers robbed some silver objects from the Lateran Basilica built by Constantine. In contrast to this policy, some secular buildings, for example on the

Santa Sabina, Rome. Built between 425 and about 433.

Forum, were severely damaged. Aurelian's old city wall which had just been reinforced could not withstand the attack. This conquest had a dramatic impact on relationships between Christians and non-Christians in Rome. Both groups were equally shocked by the disaster. The Church Father Jerome in Bethlehem said that he could not dictate to his secretary because he was weeping so much. Non-Christian dignitaries reacted similarly. Pagan senators blamed the Christians. Since Christians seized power and abolished the old religion, as when they took away the altar for Victoria, they said, Rome had declined. The neglect of the old gods led to the city's destruction.

Christians, on the other hand, claimed that it was their churches and possessions which had been spared, evidence that God supported Christianity in Rome. However, as Jerome shows, Christians were also very shaken . A theological answer to the dilemma was provided by Augustine. He wrote his 'City of God' (*De Civitate Dei*) and explained that in a Christian worldview it was not the city of

Rome that was important: the crucial issue was the city of God, the *Civitas Dei*.

Augustine finished his work in 426. At the same time the building of an outstanding church began, the church of Santa Sabina (page 152), on the Aventine Hill. The local tradition behind it told of Sabina, a second-century Roman lady who opened her private house as a meeting place for the church. Beneath the church traces of building activities from that time have been found. However, the architecture of this church made a statement that is far more important than its local tradition. It might be summed up in the slogan 'back to the roots'.

This development began with the destruction of Rome in 410. It is clear even at the entrance where a unique example of Christian art has been preserved. It is a double door with eighteen (of the original twenty-eight) pictures from the Old and New Testament carved on wooden panels. Nowhere else, not even in the catacombs, has there been a scene with so many Christian motifs. The suffering Christ on the cross is represented naked,

*D*edication by Peter the Illyrian in the church of Santa Sabina. To the left is the 'Church of the Jews' (= of the Circumcision, *Ecclesia ex circumcisione*), to the right the 'Church of the Gentiles' (= Ecclesia ex gentibus).

*C*lose up of the *Ecclesia ex circumcisione*.

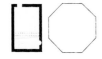

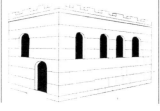

Close up of the apse mosaic of the church of Santa Pudenziana, Rome. Among other things, it shows the octagon added by Theodosius (left) to the late first century Jewish-Christian church/ synagogue on Mount Zion in Jerusalem. Compare the model sketch.

Outside wall with big stones from Herodian times which were reused here.

Model sketch of the first-century Jewish-Christian church/synago-gue.

another innovation in Christian art. The only earlier picture with this characteristic known to date is an anti-Christian graffito, a crucified man with a donkey's head, from the Palatine Hill, which dates back to the second century.

The sequence of pictures on the door depicts both Old and New Testament stories. Yet even more important is the dedicatory inscription inside the façade (page 153). It reveals a lot about Roman self-understanding after 410. Golden capital letters on a blue background describe the church's construction by Peter the Illyrian (his name is mentioned in the fourth line). The versatility of Christianity as an ideal multi-cultural society is highlighted by the two women on either side of the inscription. To the left is a typical Roman lady with an open book in her hands. The two lines below identify her as ECCLESIA EX CIR/ CUMCISIONE, 'the Church of the Circumcision' (see detail page 153). Opposite is her counterpart, the ECCLESIA EX GENTIBUS, the Church of the Gentiles. This conscious unity in diversity is expressed here for the first time.

The builder of the church came from Illyria (now in former Yugoslavia), the borderline between East and West. With the inscription and the two women on either side he demonstrated that both roots of Christianity belonged together. It may be deliberate that the women on

either side are not distinguished from one another by any cultural characteristics.

There seems to be a point of contact with a mosaic which had been designed only a few years earlier in the church of Santa Pudenziana nearby. The apse mosaic from the time of Pope Siricius (384–99) was completed by Innocent (402–17) after the conquest of Rome (page 156). Apart from Christ in the centre no other person is identified by an accompanying text. Only typical symbols of each saint lead to the conclusion that to the left Paul is depicted with a Gentile woman who crowns him with a wreath, and Peter is represented opposite with a Jewish woman. It may be supposed, then, that these women also represent the two churches, the two 'target groups' of the two apostles.

Other interpretations see the

two women as Praxidis and Potentiana, the daughters of Senator Pudens. According to a late tradition they had been baptized by Peter and Paul. However, the connection with the two women in Santa Sabina supports the previous interpretation. A further argument for this view is provided by the identification of the buildings in the background of the mosaic in Santa Pudenziana. For a long time they were understood as symbolic pictures of the 'heavenly Jerusalem'. Recently, scholars such as Gerhard Kroll and Bargil Pixner have been able to prove that those buildings relate to actual buildings in Jerusalem from Constantine's time. Left of Golgotha is the picture of the *Anastasis*, the building erected by Constantine above the empty tomb; to the right is the synagogue of Jewish Christians on Mount Zion. In front of it is the octagon built by the emperor Theodosius. Behind it is the *Eleona* church on the Mount of Olives. As at the beginning of Constantine's period, there are no buildings on the rock of Golgotha itself, probably for religious reasons.

Despite baroque alterations the structure of these mosaics is still clearly visible, so that they can be related to literary and archaeological sources. Through these connections it now seems certain that the two connected buildings to the right of Golgotha (see page 154) are the Byzantine

church of Theodosius (379–95) and the Jewish Christian late first-century synagogue. Theodosius continued Constantine's building projects, but he also corrected some abuse which had started after Christianity suddenly became so powerful. Most importantly, he counteracted isolated persecutions of Jews. On 20 September 393 (at the time when the apse mosaic in Santa Pudenziana originated) he issued a law to protect them.

His addition to the Jewish Christian synagogue on Mount Zion also fits in this context. The archaeologist and topographer Bargil Pixner has been able to show that this building (see sketch page 154) reflects a reliable local tradition that the original building contained the upper room where the Last Supper took place and the first Christian community met after Jesus' resurrection and at Pentecost. Building blocks from

Niche in the late first-century church/Jewish-Christian synagogue facing north towards Golgotha and empty tomb.

The apse mosaic in Santa Pudenziana. It was partly damaged by un-successful efforts to re-store it in the late sixteenth century.

the Herodian period incorporated in the building are important evidence for his thesis. They originally belonged to buildings destroyed by the Romans in AD70 (page 154). Further evidence for the building's Jewish origins is provided by the so-called 'Torah niche' where the scrolls of the Mosaic Law had been kept (page 155).

The niche in what has been claimed to be the tomb of David must be Christian, however, for it faces towards Golgotha and the *Anastasis*, the sites of Jesus' death and resurrection, rather than towards the temple. Therefore we can conclude that the building was constructed by Jews who had become Christians; they used the old forms of architecture, but filled them with their new faith.

The roots of Europe

We should not underestimate the fact that it is precisely this Jewish building which can be identified with one in the apse mosaic of Santa Pudenziana in Rome. After the conquest of Rome a phase of re-evaluation and re-orientation started which investigated and highlighted the Jewish heritage and origin of Christianity. This positive attitude counteracted many negative undercurrents. It was an effort to counterbalance the threat from the uncivilized barbarians by recalling all the greatness of Christian civilization and its origins. This orientation was not achieved by reinterpreting Graeco-Roman culture, as in Constantine's time. Rather, it was a direct recourse to the Old Testament and the Jewish origins of the gospel of Jesus Christ. Never before, and never since, have Christianity's Jewish origins been represented in such a positive and unbiased way in the art and architecture of official Christianity.

Santa Pudenziana, Santa Sabina, Rome and Jerusalem in the fourth and fifth centuries, highlight a cultural and humanitarian treasure which sadly has long been lost in Christian Europe, sometimes in a cruel fashion. This is also true for other countries (Spain, Switzerland and Austria, to name but a few) whose archaeological treasures have not been treated in this volume. The search for the heritage of the first Christians there has not even begun. However, it is immensely important to find, preserve and communicate this Christian heritage of our culture. It becomes all the more important the more seriously we ask ourselves whether the new Europe under the influence of the Common Market should or could again become a *Christian* Europe.